Endorsements

John Muir once wrote, "Everyone needs beauty as well as bread, places to play in and pray in, where Nature may heal and cheer and give strength to body and soul."

Betsy is one who has the gift of relating her gardening efforts to her spiritual life. There is something miraculous about watching a garden grow, green leaves bearing fruit from a seed blessed by God's gifts of sunshine and rain, tended by the dedicated efforts of a faithful and sometimes struggling human gardener. The growth of a garden is an act of grace as is our growth in our relationship to the creator of all that is. Betsy compares the various stages of gardening with her awareness of what God is teaching her about her own spiritual growth, drawing upon Bible verses that are inspiring her. Betsy's gardening is an act of prayer which she is sharing with us in her devotionals that describe what God is teaching her about the Creator and our relationship with him through her gardening. In our spiritual life, as in our gardening, we seek to tend the seeds of our faith with the understanding that both our seeds and their growth and the bearing of spiritual fruit are only reflections of God's grace, nothing we earn or deserve. It all God, all God's grace. Betsy's devotionals are an invitation for each of us to pay attention to our lives and to see and hear what God may be teaching us in his whispers to our souls.

Sandra Randleman, D.Min. Associate Pastor, First Presbyterian Church, Nashville, TN.

In her new book *Garden Devotions*, Betsy Davies gives readers inspiring paths to growth through her experiences in tilling the soil and relating that to enriching words from Scripture. I was encouraged and rewarded by her analogies, and I think you will be as well.

Etta Wilson, Agent and Editor

* * *

As plants in her own garden struggle through droughts, floods, winter freezes, and summer heat before the bountiful fruits can be harvested, Betsy Davies, an experienced gardener herself, challenges readers to see how similarly human beings struggle to bear spiritual fruit in their own lives. This Biblically based series of devotions encourages readers, not only to till the soil in their own yards, but also to trust that "He who began a good work in you will bring it to completion at the day of Christ Jesus." (Philippians 1:6)

Nan Russell

* * *

Recently, I stumbled across the phrase, "Seeds for Growth," and could not imagine a more fitting depiction for "Garden Devotions". If you are willing to be challenged to grow in your faith, be uncomfortable, a bit achy, messy, and dirty, then you have stumbled into the perfect garden! Thank you, Betsy, for this inspiring devotional which has meant more than you can possibly know to so many!

Ellie Billington, Elder, First Presbyterian Church, Nashville, TN

Garden Devotions

On God, Grief, and Growth

BETSY DAVIES

WESTBOW PRESS
A DIVISION OF THOMAS NELSON
& ZONDERVAN

Copyright © 2024 Betsy Davies.

All rights reserved. No part of this book may be used or reproduced by any means, graphic, electronic, or mechanical, including photocopying, recording, taping or by any information storage retrieval system without the written permission of the author except in the case of brief quotations embodied in critical articles and reviews.

WestBow Press books may be ordered through booksellers or by contacting:

WestBow Press
A Division of Thomas Nelson & Zondervan
1663 Liberty Drive
Bloomington, IN 47403
www.westbowpress.com
844-714-3454

Because of the dynamic nature of the Internet, any web addresses or links contained in this book may have changed since publication and may no longer be valid. The views expressed in this work are solely those of the author and do not necessarily reflect the views of the publisher, and the publisher hereby disclaims any responsibility for them.

Any people depicted in stock imagery provided by Getty Images are models, and such images are being used for illustrative purposes only. Certain stock imagery © Getty Images.

Illustrations by Linda J. Beasley

All Scripture quotations are taken from the New Revised Standard Version of the Bible, Copyright © 1989, by the Division of Christian Education of the National Council of the Churches of Christ in the United States of America. Used by permission. All rights reserved.

ISBN: 979-8-3850-2552-7 (sc)
ISBN: 979-8-3850-2553-4 (hc)
ISBN: 979-8-3850-2554-1 (e)

Library of Congress Control Number: 2024909854

Print information available on the last page.

WestBow Press rev. date: 08/13/2024

In memory of Nick and all the gardens we grew together
and
To the glory of God, the Lord Almighty,
our Father, Creator of all gardens

By contrast, the fruit of the Spirit is love, joy, peace, patience, kindness, generosity, faithfulness, gentleness, and self-control.
—Galatians 5:22

Contents

Introduction..xi

Spring Garden..................................1

Space to Grow......................................3
Till the Ground....................................5
Sugar Snap Seeds...................................7
Put Up a Fence!....................................9
The Seed and the Psalm............................11
Transformation....................................13
Thirsty?..15
Kinked Hose.......................................17
Too Many Good Things..............................19
Spring..21
Freeze Warning....................................23
Happy Place.......................................25
First Fruits......................................27
Hidden Fruit......................................31
Abundant Fruit....................................35

Summer Garden................................39

Anticipation......................................41
Starter Plants....................................43
Roots...45
Water...47
Support...49
June..51
Corralling Cucumbers..............................53
Keep Out!...55

An Unwelcome Visitor..59
Weeds 61
Waiting 65
Robbed 67
Heat of the Summer..69
Trial and Error..71
Garden Shoes..75

Autumn Harvest 79

True Beauty..81
Worth the Effort 83
Pick the Fruit..85
Bad Fruit..87
Wealth..89
Not So Fast!...91
Trapped..93
Sharing 95
Tithing 97
October 101
Pesto 103
End-Times..105
Food 107
Preparing a Feast 109
Giving Thanks..113

Winter Rest..117

Garlic Scapes..119
Ready and Waiting 121
Be Patient 123
Planning 125
Winter in the Garden.....................................127
The Heron 129
The Victory Garden..131

i and You	135
The Way of Grief	137
Busyness	139
Wind	141
Why?	143
Possibilities	147
Everything I Need	151
To Grow or Not to Grow	153
Final Thoughts	155
About the Author	157

Introduction

It was a hot August day, more than a year after my husband had died. I looked at the dying tomato and cucumber plants and wept. The dying plants seemed emblematic of so much that was wrong with my life.

Could I grow a garden without him?

My husband Nick and I had grown vegetables in our backyard for almost thirty years. Gardening was a chore and a joy we shared. Even as the cancer filled his lungs and made breathing difficult, Nick tilled the soil, put up the fencing, and planted the vegetables. Nick died in June, too soon to see the plants bear fruit. I kept the garden going in the summer after his death, but my efforts were half-hearted.

The next spring, when it was time to prepare the garden, I just didn't have the heart or the energy. I bought a couple of tomato and cucumber plants and placed them where the plants had been the year before. I didn't tend or water them regularly. They weren't thriving, and weeds overtook the garden. I used some weed killer that was supposed to be safe around vegetable plants, but it wasn't. The plants were dying. I was failing at gardening without Nick. Often, I felt I was failing at life without him.

A gentle voice in my head reminded me it was okay, even beneficial, for the ground to lie fallow for a while. Maybe I just needed to give the garden—and myself—a little time, a little grace. The grace of a garden is that I can try again next year. The grace of life is that I can start fresh each morning.

When the following spring rolled around, I set about reestablishing my garden, intentionally planning, executing, and writing about each step along the way. I wrote pages of notes and stories and insights. I realized God had long taught me lessons about life, and the Christian life in particular, through gardening.

A garden is a beautiful metaphor for the Christian life. Only God can grow the fruit, but there is so much we do that helps or hinders that growth. The garden also became a metaphor for my life as a widow. Could I continue to grow and thrive without Nick by my side? God has shown me new ways to encourage the garden to grow, new ways to foster growth in my life. God has shown me new methods and given me helpers and support.

In 2022, I began sharing my thoughts through a weekly devotional blog, www.thevictory.garden. I have gathered some of my favorites and edited them for space and content, on the following pages.

The first year I wrote, my garden was dismal. The sugar snaps didn't establish themselves; squirrels stole my tomatoes. High heat and drought challenged even my best efforts. Some of these devotionals reflect that year's garden, but others reflect on the far more successful garden I had the following year.

I have included fifteen devotionals for each season. My seasons don't follow strict guidelines but reflect patterns of behavior. I start my spring garden in late February and harvest the peas in May. I start my summer garden in late April and harvest the fruit for months. My autumn starts in late August and ends the last week of November. The number of weeks in each season varies in my life, so I have included more than the calendar gives us. Hopefully, you will find your own patterns.

A word about fruits and vegetables: Technically, anything that grows from a flower and contains a seed is a fruit. My sugar snaps, cucumbers, peppers, and tomatoes are all fruits. Roots, leaves, stems, and flowers are vegetables. The only vegetable I have in my garden is garlic. I have grown lettuce, broccoli, and carrots; those were vegetables. I interchange these words in my devotionals, as we do in everyday language.

All scripture references are NRSV. While I know that beginning with a premise and finding verses to support it can lead to bad theology and even heresy, I do not start my devotionals with a specific verse. I have found over time that much of what the Bible teaches and much of what my garden teaches fall naturally together since the same God is the source of both. An understanding of basic agricultural patterns has done much to enrich my understanding of many of the biblical verses that reference agriculture.

Now a widow, my garden does not look like the gardens Nick and I had together, but that is all right. I am learning; I am growing. My life does not look like our life together. But I am learning; I am growing. God is producing fruit in my garden and in my life. He can produce it in yours as well.

I hope you enjoy these devotionals. More importantly, I pray God speaks to you through them. God, the creator of all things, can make a plant grow from seed, can bring a body back to life, and can fill a heart with His Spirit and love.

He so wants to be in a relationship with you. He wants to grow His fruit in your life. Sow the seeds, dear friends, and watch what grows.

Betsy S. Davies

Spring Garden

Spring is a time of transformation when God brings forth plants from seeds and flowers from branches. Spring is when God gives life to what was once dead.

A farmer went out to sow his seed; and as he sowed, some fell on the path and was trampled on, and the birds of the air ate it up. Some fell on the rock; and as it grew up, it withered for lack of moisture. Some fell among thorns, and the thorns grew with it and choked it. Some fell into good soil, and when it grew, it produced a hundredfold. As he said this, he called out, "Let anyone with ears to hear listen!" (Luke 8:5–8)

Now the parable is this: The seed is the word of God. The ones on the path are those who have heard; then the devil comes and takes away the word from their hearts, so that they may not believe and be saved. The ones on the rock are those who, when they hear the word, receive it with joy. But these have no root; they believe only for a while and in a time of testing fall away. As for what fell among the thorns, these are the ones who hear; but as they go on their way, they are choked by the cares and riches and pleasures of life, and their fruit does not mature. But as for that in the good soil, these are the ones who, when they hear the word, hold it fast in an honest and good heart, and bear fruit with patient endurance. (Luke 8:11–15)

See also Matthew 13:1–23 and Mark 4:1–20.

Space to Grow

The frost has turned the brown ground gray, but green shoots are peeking through. Spots of yellow dot the creek banks. Spring is coming.

The seeds in the packet rattle as I shake them.

Will I do this? Can I do this?

I look at my garden, still brown and gray. I can almost see the sugar snaps growing there. Can you see them? Tall and green, reaching for the sun, covered with white blossoms and dangling peas. Can you taste their crisp sweetness?

Shaking the seed packet again, I make my decision. I'm planting these seeds. It will take effort on my part to prepare the ground for a garden. It will take effort and commitment to produce this fruit in my yard, to enable God to produce this fruit in my yard.

But I can see sugar snaps growing where there is only barren ground. I can taste their sweetness. I will do my part to make this vision a reality. I will give God the space needed to turn these seeds into plants, this barren ground into a garden.

While vegetables can grow anywhere, a garden is an area intentionally set aside to nurture the growth of fruit.

I wonder if God could grow His fruit in my life if I only gave Him the space to do so.

> You did not choose me but I chose you. And I appointed you to go and bear fruit, fruit that will last. (John 15:16)

I look at my life and see worries, frustrations, and petty jealousies, worthless activities inspired by a desire to impress others. Could kindness, patience, and self-control grow here? Could God grow those things in my life?

Picking up my Bible, I make my decision. I'm planting His seeds. It may well take effort on my part to prepare my life for His presence. It will take effort and commitment to enable God to produce this fruit in my life. But the vision of His love, His peace, and His joy growing in my life is just too wonderful to deny.

I want God to turn the barren and frosty ground of my life into a verdant garden bearing sweet fruit. I can almost see myself joyful and loving, reaching for the Son. I can almost taste the sweetness. Can you?

Where to start?

I look at my garden, forlorn in the backyard, resting from winter. There is space there waiting for sugar snap seeds. There is space in my life, waiting for God's Word.

> In the morning, while it was still very dark, he got up and went out to a deserted place, and there he prayed.
> (Mark 1:35)

One year, our ministers challenged the congregation to read the entire Bible in ninety days, the big read. The suggested reading path would take thirty to forty-five minutes a day, out of twenty-four hours; the equivalent of an episode of *Ozark* or *Cupcake Wars*. Could I spare the time?

What are the things that crowd my day, your day? Are you caring for your kids? Your parents? Your spouse? Yourself? Is your work schedule demanding? What are your priorities? That's really what it comes down to—what is important to you, what is important to me.

> As for me and my household, we will serve the Lord.
> (Joshua 24:15)

I can dedicate space in my yard for the sugar snaps. I can dedicate time in my day for Bible study, prayer, and praise. And I am so excited about the expected results! I can almost taste the sugar snaps. Already a smile covers my face, and His warmth is melting the frost.

Till the Ground

Before I put any seeds in the soil, I need to get the ground ready to receive them by ridding the space of rocks and weeds.

I put on my boots and long pants and drag my tiller across the yard. I crank it up and force it into the hard earth. It takes all the strength I possess to move it along the garden, ripping up weeds and turning up rocks. Often, I need help—stronger hands, arms, and backs. Tilling is arduous but rewarding at the same time. The results of my efforts are immediate.

Suddenly, the soil is darker, richer, and more receptive to new seeds, oxygen, and water. No longer is the ground hard-packed and crusty, set in its ways.

Groundbreaking is exciting. It is the herald of something new—unless, of course, you are the ground. The ground may have been perfectly happy covered in grass. I remember telling a friend of mine about a Bible study, "It will change your life!" To which she replied, "Do you think my life needs changing?" Sometimes we are happy where we are—untilled, unbroken.

But if I sow those sugar snap seeds on untilled ground, they will not take root and grow.

> A farmer went out to sow his seed, and as he sowed, some seeds fell on the path, and the birds came and ate them up. (Matthew 13:4)

While I till up the ground in my yard, I wonder if there are hard-packed areas of my life that need tilling. Where am I too resistant to the change God wants to see in me, the seeds He wants to plant? What weeds and rocks do I need to uproot and overturn? Lent, which providentially coincides with the tilling season, provides the perfect excuse for such self-examination.

> See now, I am for you; I will turn to you, and you shall
> be tilled and sown. (Ezekiel 36:9)

Sometimes I till myself to open my life up to God, and sometimes I feel tilled against my will. The year 2020 was such a time for a lot of us; COVID-19 ripped up our lives and overturned our plans against our wishes. Has COVID-19 opened you up to something new, or has the grass grown back?

If we ever want to grow something new, we need to prepare ourselves for God's presence because God works best in our lives when we, like the soil in the garden, are tilled and broken.

> The sacrifice acceptable to God is a broken spirit;
> a broken and contrite heart, O God, you will not
> despise. (Psalm 51:17)

Perhaps it is my pride and self-centeredness that I need to break. Perhaps it is my attachment to earthly pleasures, worldly success, and others' approval. Perhaps it is my "self" that I am called to crucify daily (Luke 9:23) so that I can follow Jesus.

If we follow the verbs used in the feeding of the five thousand (Mark 6:41) and the Last Supper (Matthew 26:26)—take, bless, break, and give—then we must be broken before God can share us with others.

So grab your tiller and join me. Let's break some ground.

Sugar Snap Seeds

Holding the sugar snap seeds in the palm of my hand, I look at the picture on the cover of the package. These seeds will produce this beautiful fruit? My cynical side finds that difficult to believe.

Why do I tamp down my expectations like this? Has God not shown us over thousands of years that He will turn these dried-out pods into plants? Has He not shown me and others just how big the plants these seeds contain can become? I have instructions, directions, and testimonies from others. Why do I doubt it? One thing is for sure: if I don't plant them, they will remain only seeds.

To look at these little dried peas and see a six-foot plant covered with white blossoms and sugar snaps—is that not faith?

> Now faith is the assurance of things hoped for, the conviction of things not seen. (Hebrews 11:1)

Every tree in my yard started as a seed. Every tree in your yard started as a seed—a seed that looked absolutely nothing like the tree it became. A forest is a testimony to God's ability to transform something seemingly dead into something vibrantly alive.

These dried peas in the palm of my hand hold the promise of transforming my garden. Amazing, really—and so common. You can find these packets of hope in every hardware store and garden center in the world.

These little seeds, these embodiments of hope, energize me at some deep level.

They appear dead, dried up, lifeless, worthless. But looks can be deceiving.

These dead-looking, dried-up peas are precious to me. These seeds hold the promise of delicious fruit. It doesn't always work out that way, but while you may see a dried-up seed, I see possibility.

> The Lord does not see as mortals see; they look on the outward appearance, but the Lord looks on the heart.
> (1 Samuel 16:7)

I feel like the dried-up snow pea seed at times: insignificant, useless, past my prime. My cynical nature doubts there is much that can come from me; my fears and doubts tamp down my expectations. But I must fight these fears.

God creates form from nothing (Genesis 1), brings dead bones to life (Ezekiel 37), plants an imperishable seed within us (1 Peter 1), and promises resurrection (1 Corinthians 15). Surely, He can transform me into a fruit-bearing garden.

So I plant these seeds. I water them, tend to them, protect them, and support them. I trust God will transform them. He has been faithful in the past, transforming millions of seeds into flowers, plants, and trees. I have faith that He can and will transform these seeds, and me, as well.

> Beloved, we are God's children now; what we will be has not yet been revealed. What we do know is this: when he is revealed, we will be like him, for we will see him as he is. (1 John 3:2)

What hope these little seeds carry!
It may look like a little seed, but it is so much more.

> He said therefore, "What is the kingdom of God like? And to what shall I compare it? It is like a mustard seed that someone took and sowed in the garden; it grew and became a tree, and the birds of the air made nests in its branches." (Luke 13:18–19)

Put Up a Fence!

As I put my first seeds in the ground, it's as if an alarm sounds, the puck drops, and the ball is tossed at center court. I am in battle. The birds watch me intently from their perches, the bunnies peer longingly from the hedges, the neighbor's dog strains at her leash; even the grass seems to lean in as if to recover lost territory. They covet the seeds, the young plants, the fertile ground.

No! Stay away! This is *my* garden. This is the space I have set aside, and you are not welcome here. This is not unkind or selfish: The birds and bunnies have the rest of the yard. The dog can play elsewhere. The grass has plenty of territory. I have dedicated this space to nurturing those sugar snap seeds into fruit-bearing plants. They need to stay out; I need a fence.

I have over 150 yards of wire fencing in manageable segments, folded and flattened in my garage. I take what I need into the yard, unfold, and re-flatten it by stepping on it, then stretch it between the poles around my seeds. It's my own personal workout session—works the legs and the arms! The fence keeps most two- and four-legged creatures from invading my garden. I even cover the seeded area—birds love those seeds!

> Listen to another parable. There was a landowner who planted a vineyard, put a fence around it, dug a winepress in it, and built a watchtower. (Matthew 21:33)

I went to a youth service once where they asked us to leave our cell phones at the door; the chapel was a space set aside to honor God. Same idea.

When you have set aside a time to meet with God, when you have prepared your heart to receive the seeds He's planting, protect that space from predators and invaders. Turn off the phone, turn off the TV, and train your brain to stay in the moment. Use the tools available—the Bible, a journal, a devotional book, an inspirational book, whatever it takes to give God a dedicated space in your life.

Sometimes that takes saying no. Jesus did.

> At daybreak he departed and went into a deserted place. And the crowds were looking for him; and when they reached him, they wanted to prevent him from leaving them. But he said to them, "I must proclaim the good news of the kingdom of God to other cities also, for I was sent for this purpose." (Luke 4:42–43)

Saying no is not always selfish or lazy; sometimes it is prioritizing God's will for my life. Sometimes saying no is a way to keep the predators and invaders out.

The image of a stone garden wall comes to mind. Stone walls were the traditional barriers around gardens and homes, towns, and temples. To make the walls, the builders carefully place each stone one upon the other.

If I am a temple of the Holy Spirit, as Paul asserts in 1 Corinthians 6:19, then I should protect that temple at least as much as I protect my garden. Each Bible verse that I memorize and internalize becomes a stone that builds up the wall protecting the Holy Spirit's residence in my life. Each verse is a stone carefully placed one upon another. That protective stone wall enables the Holy Spirit to produce fruit in my life. And that is a beautiful thing.

Are you protecting your garden? Are you keeping the invaders and predators out? Are you building up your garden wall with stones of faith? I encourage you to join me in this effort.

It can be a workout, but it's worth it.

The Seed and the Psalm

The little sugar snap seeds are in the ground. I must let them sit in the dirt; I must wait for the weather and God to transform them. There is little I can do to speed up the process or even check on it. This transformation from seed to sprout is something that must go on inside the seed as it sits alone in the dark soil.

I have felt like that little seed before—covered with dirt, alone in the dark.

Even when there were those who cared for me and made sure I had sunlight and water, I was not sure that I would ever become more than the lifeless shell I was at that moment.

> I am weary with my moaning; every night I flood my bed with tears; I drench my couch with weeping.
> (Psalm 6:6)

In grief counseling, my pastor had me write a psalm. I found it the other day, folded and hidden away in my Bible. The paper was still crisp and clean, untouched and avoided. Perhaps the pain expressed in it needed time, just as my sugar snap seeds do.

Even as I read the words now, the back of my throat constricts and tears form. How can this still hurt so much?

There is hope hidden in the pain, a willingness to let God lead me out of the darkness. There is faith that a plant will grow, but that space is dark and lonely.

I thought I would share it with you, maybe expose this dark space to a little light.

"Betsy's Psalm of Lament" (1/25/20)

> You are with me, Lord, but this is hard.
> It hurts my heart, my soul, my body.
> It challenges who I am.

> You must have some plan, some good in mind,
> but how will You bring *joy* out of *this*?
> How long will this hurt?
> > How long before I feel joy? Or love?
> > How long before "normal" returns to me?
> > It all feels so wrong without him.
> > It is tempting to just give up, give in, to shut the door, lock myself in, and die.
> But I will trust in You, Lord.
> > I will turn my face to You and see Your presence all around me.
> > I will open the door and go outside this painful space.
> > You have surrounded me with friends.
> > I will let them hold me, and I will sing Your praise.

We are so uncomfortable around grief, around pain. If expressed too openly, we doubt its authenticity. We fear doing or saying the wrong thing, adding insult to injury. We don't have the words to express grief or comfort the grieving. Odd, since we have all experienced loss since childhood. How has the loss of a toy, a pet, a grandparent, not trained us for the loss of a dream, a parent, or a spouse? Why do I find my own pain so difficult to expose? Is not grief as common as seeds in the ground?

I have left that very dark space. God has surrounded me with the warmth of friends, the light of His Word, and the life-giving water of prayer. The seed of grief *did* crack open, allowing a tender sprout to reach for the sun, reach for the Son.

Amazing.

> A new heart I will give you, and a new spirit I will put within you; and I will remove from your body the heart of stone and give you a heart of flesh. (Ezekiel 36:26)

Transformation

I stare at the ground. Is anything happening? It doesn't look like anything is happening. I vaguely remember learning about the germination process. If I put the seed into an environment of tilled soil, ample water, and sufficient nutrients, it will come alive, send down roots, and push a sprout through the dirt, reaching for the sun.

Supposedly. I can't see it. I can't really dig up the ground and check. If it's happening, it's happening in secret.

> But whenever you pray, go into your room and shut the door and pray to your Father who is in secret; and your Father who sees in secret will reward you. (Matthew 6:6)

Transformation does not occur through the constant barrage of media, my tireless pursuit of entertainment, or my endless activities. Transformation occurs underground, out of sight, in secret.

It is only when I spend time in quiet, with God in secret, that He can transform the little seed of me into a better me.

> And all of us, with unveiled faces, seeing the glory of the Lord as though reflected in a mirror, are being transformed into the same image from one degree of glory to another; for this comes from the Lord, the Spirit. (2 Corinthians 3:18)

Transformation happens in the quiet, undisturbed soil of my soul.

In my garden, my sugar snap seeds need an area safe from predators and the elements to first break open their hard shells and expose the fragile tendrils within. The emerging plant needs some undisturbed time to allow its roots to search out the depths before it can think about surfacing. And even then, the transformed seed needs to mature a little before it pushes through the soil to expose itself to the world.

And what a glorious moment that is! Those first little sprigs of sugar snap plants bursting through the ground. Wow! There is joy in every single one of them. Don't you think God is just as joyful when we allow ourselves to be transformed into all He created us to be?

> Just so, I tell you, there will be more joy in heaven over one sinner who repents than over ninety-nine righteous persons who need no repentance. (Luke 15:7)

Have you ever sensed God has changed your attitude about someone or something? I have, and it happened in the quiet times of prayer and communion with God—underground, out of the eye of the public. I doubt anyone else even noticed the change, the transformation at first. Then those first little sprigs of change burst from my hardened heart. Wow!

I only need to put the little seed of myself into God's hands—go into my room, shut the door, and pray to my Father in secret. And the God who sees in secret will reward me by transforming me more into His likeness.

Thirsty?

I wonder if I look silly watering the dirt in my garden. Maybe the fence will let others know that I am trying to grow something in this space, even if there is no evidence of it yet. Every day, I go out to my garden and water the dirt there.

I know there are seeds in the ground, and if I want the seeds to become plants and bear fruit, I must water them. This is not some suggestion for a healthier plant; this is the difference between life and death for my plant. Water does not provide an additional benefit for my growing plant; water is essential.

Without water, that dried-up seed remains a dried-up seed. Without water, the flower inside that tiny seed never bursts from its shell and reaches for the sun. Without water, that seed never becomes a plant, never grows, and never bears fruit.

Plants know they need water. They send roots deep into the ground to search for it. The trees near my creek send their roots toward the water there, breaking through the banks to find this precious resource.

Sometimes, it rains. Water comes from the heavens to nourish and transform my plants. Especially in the spring, we can expect rain on a regular basis. It's as if God knew these deceptively dead plants need water to transform into healthy plants.

But I don't depend on rain to water my garden as it grows. I am grateful when it rains; I am grateful when the watering of my garden happens naturally, spontaneously, without effort on my part. But on those days when the rain doesn't come, I get out the hose.

I know that as the plants grow, the need for water increases. Daily, I must get out the hose and water my garden because water is mandatory if I want my garden to survive, if I want my garden to thrive, if I want my garden to produce.

> Then Jesus told them a parable about their need to pray always and not to lose heart. (Luke 18:1)

Prayer is like water to those who want to grow in their spiritual faith. Prayer is not some suggestion for a healthier faith; it is essential. Without prayer, my dried-up spirit remains dried up. Without prayer, the flower inside my soul never bursts from its shell and reaches for the sun. Without prayer, that seed of faith never becomes a plant, never grows, and never bears fruit.

> Do not worry about anything, but in everything by prayer and supplication with thanksgiving let your requests be made known to God. (Philippians 4:6)

Sometimes prayer seems to leap spontaneously from my heart. Often these are prayers of praise and thanks; sometimes these are prayers of anguish and distress, or of concern and fear. I am always grateful when prayer happens spontaneously, without effort on my part. But on those days when the prayers don't come on their own, I get on my knees.

I know that as my faith grows, my need for prayer increases. Daily, I must set aside time to pray, to commune with God, to bring Him all my concerns, and to listen to all He has to tell me.

Because prayer is mandatory if I want my faith to survive, if I want my faith to thrive, if I want my faith to produce.

> Devote yourselves to prayer, keeping alert in it with thanksgiving. (Colossians 4:2)

As I water the dirt in my garden, I can sense the seeds sending their roots deeper, anchoring them in place. I can sense the young sprouts bursting from the seeds, breaking through their hard shells, and heading for the light. This is joy; this is hope.

I will remember to water today; my soul is thirsty.

Kinked Hose

It seemed like the perfect day. I could feel the warm sun on my face and the gentle breeze ruffling through my hair. The hedgerow was in bloom, sending fragrant scents across the yard. My sugar snaps were up. I held the hose and gently sprayed water on the green plants.

Then suddenly, there was no water. I was standing there holding the hose, pressing the handle, but nothing was happening. I turned and looked at the hose, stretched out on the ground. Sure enough, it had twisted, creating a kink that blocked the flow of water. Never once did I think that there was no water to be had. The water was there; a kink in the hose was blocking it.

Why, then, when my prayers seem unanswered and my cries seem to fall on deaf ears, do I presume God has turned away and is not listening? Instead of thinking that God has stopped the flow of water, shouldn't I first look for the blockage on my end?

> You ask and do not receive, because you ask wrongly,
> in order to spend what you get on your pleasures.
> (James 4:3)

For the past few weeks, every time I settle into a prayer time, I remember a particular person and think I should reach out to her. For some reason I can't explain, I have yet to do so. So this morning, before I prayed, I wrote her a note and put it in the mailbox. It seems pointless to pray for God's direction when I do not follow the instructions He gives me. Perhaps this small act of obedience will unblock the hose and allow the Spirit a larger presence in my life.

> So when you are offering your gift at the altar, if you remember that your brother or sister has something against you, leave your gift there before the altar and

> go; first be reconciled to your brother or sister, and then come and offer your gift. (Matthew 5:23–24)

God hears every prayer. God stands ready to pour out His presence into our lives. While God can block the flow of water to accomplish His end (think Moses), these seem to be rare occurrences. It seems more likely that *we* are blocking the flow; we have twisted and constricted ourselves, preventing God from flowing through us.

Consider too that what we ask may be outside God's plan. God has a much bigger picture than we do; He sees all people at all times in all places. He sees the unseen battles waged among us. Would not each of us have prayed that Jesus be spared His misery at the hands of the Roman soldiers? Did not even Jesus pray this? But there was more at stake than Jesus's comfort. Prayer is not about getting God to do what we want Him to do; prayer is not about getting God to do *our* will.

> Abba, Father, for you all things are possible; remove this cup from me; yet not what I want, but what you want. (Mark 14:36)

I shake the hose. When that doesn't work, I find the kink in the hose and untwist it. I stop wasting time holding a blocked hose and correct the situation so the water will flow. How easy that seems in the garden; how difficult that seems sometimes in my prayer life.

The water flows freely now. The plants are getting their life-giving moisture. They are thriving. God is amazing, is He not?

Hopefully, the water is flowing freely in your life. If not, perhaps take a moment today to review your situation and unkink the hose.

Too Many Good Things

Green sprouts are bursting from the ground. The sugar snaps are up, pushing up through the soil, welcomed by sunshine and rain! Yay! Especially after last year when so few seeds germinated.

Since last year's crop was sparse, I planted a whole bunch of seeds this year, far more than recommended, hoping for more seeds to sprout.

And God, with His unique sense of humor, had them *all* sprout. Too many good things.

There is not adequate space between the plants for them all to grow well. They may grow tall, but there is not enough space for them to spread out their fruit-bearing branches. In advertising, we call the space between things "white space." The white space is almost as important as the wording; the white space allows us to read the wording and clues us into its interpretation.

The plants need this white space, this space between, as well: space for the sunlight to reach the leaves, space for the branches to reach out and grow, and space for the roots to establish themselves in the soil.

> At daybreak he departed and went into a deserted place.
> And the crowds were looking for him. (Luke 4:42)

I am going to have to thin my sugar snap plants. It's a difficult thing to do, because I want all of them. But I know that some of them will have to go if I want the rest of them to be successful; if I leave them all, none of them will grow well.

I am facing a similar dilemma in my life right now. I had a busy life pre-COVID. During the COVID-19 pandemic, I developed some new patterns and activities that are dear to me. Now all the old activities are back as well, and I have new grand-twins.

Too many good things.

There is not adequate space for me to do all these things well. I need some white space; I need some space between.

It may seem counterintuitive, but in the face of too much to do, I am observing the Jewish Sabbath for Lent. I imposed some white space on my life. I have found that it helps me focus on what's important; it allows me to pay attention to God and what He wants me to do.

Observing a twenty-four-hour no-work zone has also encouraged me to work more efficiently during the other six days. I find I am wasting less time on the other days. It is forcing me to be intentional about how I am spending my time.

> Finally, beloved, whatever is true, whatever is honorable, whatever is just, whatever is pure, whatever is pleasing, whatever is commendable, if there is any excellence and if there is anything worthy of praise, think about these things. (Philippians 4:8)

So don't ask me about the latest murder trial; I am not filling my space with that. I am leaving uncluttered space for the plants I want to grow, space for the sunlight to reach the leaves, space for the branches to reach out and grow, and space for the roots to establish themselves in the soil.

Because God is growing something in my life and in yours. We just need to make room for it to grow, even if it means getting rid of some good things.

Be still and know that I am God! (Psalm 46:10)

Create some space, my friend. If you are not sure which plants to thin or which good thing to eliminate, ask God for guidance. And take time to listen for His answer.

Spring

What a glorious time of year this is! As I check on my growing sugar snaps, I feel the warm sun on my shoulders and the slight breeze across my face. I can smell the damp earth and see the green leaves peeping out of what once looked like dead tree limbs. A mockingbird is serenading me with his friends' favorite songs. And the best of all, Christ is risen!

Martin Luther's biographer credits him with saying, "Our Lord has written the promise of resurrection, not in books alone, but in every leaf in springtime." Is it merely a coincidence that Passover, and therefore Easter, takes place in spring? I think not!

Spring, when God brings the dead trees to life, leads his people out of slavery, and transforms sinners into heirs of His kingdom through the death and resurrection of Jesus.

> But to all who received him, who believed in his name,
> he gave power to become children of God. (John 1:12)

Spring is all about transformation. As a gardener, I get to witness the amazing transformation from seed to plant in my backyard. As a lover of the outdoors, I get to see the barren limbs of trees transform into a canopy of green leaves. Sleeping plants awaken and push through the thawing ground; buds appear on the end of limbs and burst into color. Baby bunnies appear in the yard with their parents, and nests once holding eggs now hold chirping balls of fuzz.

Spring brings Easter when God ushered in the ultimate transformation. Jesus's resurrection from the dead ushered in the Holy Spirit's presence in the lives of believers, transforming us into His image, His children, His body. God is making us a new creation (2 Corinthians 5:17), giving us a new heart and a new spirit (Ezekiel

36:26), and transforming us into His likeness (1 John 3:2). What a glorious time of year this is!

And this week, the week before Easter, Holy Week, encourages us to see how much we need God to transform us. We see the joy and the praise, but we also see the dirt and the struggle. We, like the garden, like all disciples everywhere, have days of growth and days of denial. We have to admit that there are difficult times, pain, disappointment, even what looks like failure. But Easter is coming.

New growth is coming. Transformation is coming. His kingdom is coming.

To bury a seed and watch it become a plant and bear fruit—what a gift! To see the stump of a bush or the twigs of a tree produce a leaf, a bud, a flower—amazing! If nothing else, gardening makes me go outside and see the evidence of God and His transforming power.

> For what can be known about God is plain to them, because God has shown it to them. Ever since the creation of the world, his eternal power and divine nature, invisible though they are, have been understood and seen through the things he has made. (Romans 1:19–20)

I encourage you this week to go outside and stand in your yard, or a park if you don't have a yard. Feel the sun on your shoulders and the breeze on your face. Listen to the birds sing their praises. You can almost feel the earth coming alive. You can almost see resurrection in a leaf.

He is risen! He is risen indeed!

Freeze Warning

It's cold outside today. It's been cold for a few days now, and the forecaster says it's getting colder. "Cover your plants!" In case I haven't been paying attention, my sister calls to make sure I know. Several friends mention the freeze warning and ask if I'm worried.

Sugar snaps and their snow pea cousins do well in cool weather. It's hot weather they don't like. That's why gardeners plant them in February and March. I am pretty sure my growing plants can withstand the temperatures dropping below 32, pretty sure.

I heed the warnings and cover the plants. Even though the forecasters often get it wrong. Even though the sugar snaps should withstand the cold.

Covering the plants carries its own risks and takes effort. I use a floating cover, of which I have a limited supply, because it allows for more airflow than old sheets, of which I have plenty. It's also lighter, so less likely to damage the plants, but more likely to blow away if not secured.

It's difficult to know just what the best course of action is.

> We must no longer be children, tossed to and fro and blown about by every wind of doctrine. (Ephesians 4:14)

I have had gardens for over thirty years, and I still don't know if I am being fearful or prudent.

Fear seems to be the currency of the day. The news seems to peddle it as arduously as any snake-oil salesman. The sky is falling! Russia, China, the economy, school shootings, domestic terrorists, foreign terrorists, plagues, cyber and biological warfare—sometimes I wonder if I should leave the house!

> And you will hear of wars and rumors of wars; see that you are not alarmed; for this must take place, but the end is not yet. For nation will rise against nation, and kingdom against kingdom, and there will be famines and earthquakes in various places: all this is but the beginning of the birth-pangs. (Matthew 24:6–8)

I will not be alarmed, but I will be prudent. I will take precautions; I will cover my plants.

Because plants are living things, and God has entrusted their care to me. These specific plants are my responsibility. I want to be a good steward; I want these plants in my care to thrive.

Even if I think they may be fine without my help, why take that chance? Why not make their lives a little easier for the next few days? Why not give them the equivalent of a blanket or a hug?

Last week, a friend of mine had a medical scare. Another friend was right there with her, following her home, calling the ambulance, making sure she was okay, and caring for her. Perhaps she would have been fine without help; perhaps she could have gotten herself to the hospital and home, but I am so glad that our friend was there to help her through the scary forecast.

And aren't we all called to do that for one another?

> I give you a new commandment, that you love one another. Just as I have loved you, you also should love one another. By this everyone will know that you are my disciples, if you have love for one another. (John 13:34–35)

Yes, it took some effort to cover my sugar snaps, but I did not panic about the potential of freezing temperatures. I trust I am listening to the warnings and acting with my plants' best interest in mind.

I hope I can be that caring for all of God's creation, even perhaps you. Do you need a blanket? Or a hug? Do you know someone who does?

Happy Place

The sugar snaps are back in their happy place.

Nick and I always planted the sugar snaps at the far-left end of the garden. After his death, I condensed the garden and planted them at the far-right end. The creek rose three feet that year, taking most of the plants with it. Last year I moved them out of flood threat, but not to their original location. Crop rotation, you know. They didn't like that space. This year they are back in their happy place.

What joy it brings me to see them thriving! It has been several years since I have had any sugar snaps to harvest, but I am feeling very optimistic about this year.

We all know that we are to bloom where we are planted, make the best of an unpleasant situation, and use every situation as an opportunity to glorify God, but let's admit it. Most of us have a happy place, a place where growth seems easy and life is good and praise leaps to our lips without effort.

As much as it is in our ability to do so, I think we should put ourselves in our happy place. If hiking in the woods makes you happy, leave the laundry for later and take a walk. If holding that baby fills you with joy, respond to your emails later. If a walk on the beach brings you closer to God, figure out a way to get there.

> But the Lord answered her, "Martha, Martha, you are worried and distracted by many things; there is need for only one thing." (Luke 10:41)

I have found great joy writing these posts. I have found great joy thinking about what I am writing in these posts. I have found joy thinking about God and specifically about my relationship with God, my garden, if you will. Thinking about and writing these posts has become a happy place, where I let the other things fade away.

Do you have a happy place? A place where you feel closer to God, a time when the cares of the world fade in the background and communion with God seems easier? Perhaps it is time with a beloved friend or quiet time with your spouse. Perhaps looking at water puts everything in perspective. Perhaps it is a steady jog on a well-known path.

God has filled the earth with happy places for His creation. The sugar snaps were not happy in the area where I usually grow cucumbers or in the area where I normally grow peppers. They have their own happy place, at the far-left end of the garden. The actual place is not nearly as important as that there we meet God, commune with Him, and worship Him.

> Woman, believe me, the hour is coming when you will worship the Father neither on this mountain nor in Jerusalem ... True worshipers will worship the Father in spirit and truth, for the Father seeks such as these to worship him. (John 4:21, 4:23)

Sometimes gardening is just such a happy place. Admittedly, sometimes it is a place of hard work, struggle, and frustration. Perhaps there is a lesson there as well.

Many of our happy places are not always happy. It takes effort to hike. Sometimes the baby screams. Sand can be hard to walk in. The words don't come. Friends and spouses argue. Storms obscure your view of the water. Muscles cramp when you jog. But when I see those glorious sugar snaps, somehow the effort and failures fade into the background.

> I am confident of this, that the one who began a good work among you will bring it to completion by the day of Jesus Christ. (Philippians 1:6)

May you, like my sugar snaps, find your happy place.

First Fruits

There is fruit on the vine—sugar snap pods hang from the little white flowers! What a cause for celebration!

These are the first fruits of my garden.

> You shall take some of the first of all the fruit of the ground which you harvest from the land that God is giving you, and you shall put it in a basket and go to the place that the Lord your God will choose. Then you, along with the Levites and the aliens who reside among you, shall celebrate with all the bounty that the Lord your God has given to you and your house. (Deuteronomy 26:2, 26:11)

Moses established an annual celebration for the people of God to thank the Lord for His provision and celebrate with those who couldn't provide for themselves. I shared mine with some Christian women with no gardens.

I love that my peas ripen during the period the Jews celebrate as the Festival of Weeks, the seven weeks between Passover and Pentecost. When exactly one makes the firstfruits offering during this period is unclear. Many have it occur on the first day of the week after Passover—that would be Easter Sunday.

> But in fact Christ has been raised from the dead, the first fruits of those who have died. (1 Corinthians 15:20)

But one could make their firstfruits offering any time during the seven weeks, even as late as Pentecost, when Jews celebrated the gift of the law in addition to the gift of fruit—Pentecost, when God gave us the gift of the Holy Spirit as well.

> We ourselves, who have the first fruits of the Spirit, groan inwardly while we wait for adoption, the redemption of our bodies. (Romans 8:23)

So Christ is the first fruit, and we who abide in Him are also first fruits. What a cause for celebration! The Lord our God has certainly provided all that we need!

Since I can't share my sugar snaps with you personally, I want to share something else. God provides for us and asks that we share His provision with others. That certainly refers to His physical provision, but I think it also refers to His spiritual provision. We are to tell our stories.

"What a Wonderful God" by Betsy Davies

> I am a woman, come down from the mountain to tell my story, a story of the majesty and the wonder of God. How glorious it is on the mountain! Surrounded by endless sky, the stars seem close enough to touch. Pure crisp air fills my lungs; and the joy of God's presence fills my soul. He takes my hand and leads me.
>
> > What a wonderful God He is, to bring me to this place, to show me His glory, to call me by name. What a wonderful God!
>
> I am a woman, come up from the pit to tell my story, a story of the grace and mercy of God. How gentle He is with my pain, how tender He is as I weep from my heart. He comforts me as my guilt and doubt and fear shred me to pieces. His presence heals my wounds. He takes my hand and leads me.
>
> > What a wonderful God He is, to bring me out of this place, to show me His gracious love, to call me by name. What a wonderful God!

I am a woman, come across the plain to tell my story, a story of the support and providence of God. He provides fresh water and rest along the way. He keeps me on the path and carries my load. Walking through hidden rocks and fragrant flowers, wearied by the endless vistas, He whispers, "There is better ahead." He takes my hand and leads me.

What a wonderful God He is, to walk with me through this place, to show me His faithfulness, to call me by name. What a wonderful God!

Happy Pentecost, you first fruits of the Spirit! I am grateful for you!

Hidden Fruit

Tiny white blossoms show themselves against the verdant green of the healthy sugar snaps plants. I know each blossom yields a dangling pea pod, but those green pods are much harder to see.

A few are right there on the end of the little branch, proudly declaring themselves, but most of them hide behind stems and leaves, worried about the bright sun and marauding birds, too timid and embarrassed to expose themselves.

I have a trick for getting this fruit to show. Gently shake the plant. The sugar snaps react differently to the shaking than the leaves and stems do. They sway differently. Your eye, if you are looking, sees the difference at once.

The Holy Spirit, bearing His fruit in our lives, allows us to react differently as well. When God gently shakes our world, our reactions differ from those of the nonbelievers around us.

> Blessed are you when people revile you and persecute you and utter all kinds of evil against you falsely on my account. Rejoice and be glad, for your reward is great in heaven, for in the same way they persecuted the prophets who were before you. (Matthew 5:11–12)

Perhaps our world just needs a little shaking for our fruit to show up.

I must admit I would rather the shaking not be necessary. I would rather the fruit be obvious. Oddly enough, even then, it is sometimes hard to see.

Sometimes I don't see the fruit that is right in front of my eyes. Sometimes I don't see my keys sitting on the table, or the mayo in the fridge. What is it that makes me not see the thing right in front of my eyes? Is my mind preoccupied with other thoughts? Am I so stressed about looking for it that I'm temporarily blinded? Am I running some visual tape from the past instead of actually looking at the present view? Do I do this with issues far more important than mayo or keys or peas?

> You will indeed listen, but never understand, and you will indeed look, but never perceive. For this people's heart has grown dull, and their ears are hard of hearing, and they have shut their eyes; so that they might not look with their eyes, and listen with their ears, and understand with their heart and turn—and I would heal them. (Matthew 13:14–15, Acts 28:26, Isaiah 6:10, Jeremiah 5:21, Ezekiel 12:2)

Somehow, we can tell when we are looking and *seeing*.

We can tell when others are *seeing* us; we can sense it when we are talking to them.

I can only imagine what it must have felt like to have Jesus concentrate his gaze on you. Whether you were a rich young ruler (Mark 10:21), a tax collector (Luke 19:5), a fisherman (Matthew 4:18), or a denying disciple (Luke 22:61), when Jesus looked at you, when Jesus saw you, he saw what was really there. Not blinded by outward appearances, societal norms, or preconceived notions, Jesus looked and saw.

Jesus can see the Holy Spirit's fruit growing in our lives. God can give us this type of sight as well. We can see God around us. We can see His fruit in others; we can see His fruit in ourselves.

> So have no fear of them; for nothing is covered up that will not be uncovered, and nothing secret that will not become known. What I say to you in the dark, tell in the light; and what you hear whispered proclaim from the rooftops. (Matthew 10:26–27)

These verses aren't talking about the shameful things we try to hide; these verses are talking about the fruit that God is bearing in our lives, the tender moments when He heals our pain and takes our hand. When God is bearing fruit in your life, some of it will be obvious, but some may hide, camouflaged by our daily lives. So don't worry when God shakes your life a little; He's just making His fruit obvious to the world.

Abundant Fruit

The sugar snaps are thriving. I am picking nearly one hundred sweet peas every day. They are so delicious and such a treat to share them with family and friends! There are certainly too many for me to eat by myself.

Friends have asked why this crop has been so good when last year's was so bad. Of course, there is no single answer to that question, but "right time, right place" seems to sum it up.

Last year, spring was hot and dry. This spring has been cool and rainy, ideal for the peas.

This year, I planted my seeds in their happy place, perhaps because the soil contains the right nutrients, perhaps because the hedgerow blocks the afternoon sun. Maybe there was a lesson I needed to learn from the failed crop last year. Whatever the reason, I am overwhelmed with gratitude for the abundant harvest this year.

Sometimes, there is a "right time, right place" for what God calls us to do as well. We may not understand why we need to do whatever it is God is calling us to do today and not tomorrow, but if God calls us to do it today, then today is when we should do it.

In Deuteronomy 1, God tells his people to enter the Promised Land. Afraid, they delay their obedience. When Moses chastises them, they decide to obey the earlier command, but the moment for obedience has passed. Their delay results in a rout, followed by forty years of wandering.

> Although I told you, you would not listen. You rebelled against the command of the Lord and presumptuously went up into the hill country. (Deuteronomy 1:43)

Compare this failure to the battle of Jericho, where the people follow God's unusual and illogical commands exactly, resulting in a tremendous victory (Joshua 6).

I love the image of the walls just falling down without human effort. It gives me hope when I look at some of the supposedly insurmountable problems facing us today.

This year's thriving sugar snaps, after last year's failure, also give me hope. What happened last year does not dictate what can happen this year. Our past need not determine our future; if we obey God, anything can happen. Four years ago, my life was falling apart as I walked my husband through his last month on earth. Who could have predicted that this year I would rejoice over an abundant sugar-snap harvest?

Who could have predicted this amazing harvest? I did not even hope for such a crop. I prepared the ground, planted the seeds, tended the plants, and let God provide. And boy, has He!

In fact, the abundant fruit has caused a problem. The plants have grown taller than expected and are taller than my support cages. Laden with the relatively heavy ripe fruit, the tops of the plants are falling over. Such abundant fruit needs better support. Gently, I am trying to encourage the plants to stay upright and not become entangled. Next year, I will provide taller supports, but for this year, I can only try to lessen the stress on the plant.

The best way to do this is to pick the peas. As I break off the ripe fruit, the branch lifts, its burden removed.

Can the fruit God's Spirit produces in us become a burden for us as well? If we retain our grasp on it and do not share it with others, will it weigh us down, hinder our growth and entangle us? Is love really love if we do not give it to others? What about gentleness and patience? Doesn't God give us gifts precisely so that we will share them with others?

> I will bless you and make your name great, so that you will be a blessing. (Genesis 12:2)

Like good stewards of the manifold grace of God, serve one another with whatever gift each of you has received. (1 Peter 4:10)

God can produce an abundant harvest in you, in the right place, at the right time. If He is, take the time today to share your abundance with others.

Summer Garden

Summer is a time of growth when God encourages plants to strengthen and mature. Summer is when God produces fruit.

I am the true vine, and my father is the vinegrower. He removes every branch in me that bears no fruit. Every branch that bears fruit he prunes to make it bear more fruit. You have already been cleansed by the word that I have spoken to you. Abide in me as I abide in you. Just as the branch cannot bear fruit by itself unless it abides in the vine, neither can you unless you abide in me. I am the vine; you are the branches. Those who abide in me and I in them bear much fruit, because apart from me you can do nothing. Whoever does not abide in me is thrown away like a branch and withers; such branches are gathered, thrown into the fire, and burned. If you abide in me, and my words abide in me, ask for whatever you wish, and it will be done for you. My Father is glorified by this, that you bear much fruit and become my disciples. As the Father has loved me, so I have loved you; abide in my love. If you keep my commandments, you will abide in my love just as I have kept my Father's commandments and abide in his love. I have said these things to you so that my joy may be in you, and that your joy may be complete. This is my commandment, that you love one another as I have loved you. (John 15:1–12)

If you follow my statutes and keep my commandments and observe them faithfully, I will give you your rains in their season, and the land shall yield its produce, and the trees of the field shall yield their fruit. (Leviticus 26:3–4)

Anticipation

Black weed cloth covers newly tilled soil, and the scent of dirt is still strong. The garden is ready for its summer plants. We had a wonderful time getting it ready.

My daughter, son-in-law, and grandbabies, along with my ever-helpful brother-in-law, joined me in preparing the space. We took turns caring for the babies as we tilled and raked the summer garden. We set up a watering system with multiple soaker hoses in addition to the hose for hand watering. We laid down weed barrier cloth and covered it with mulch, finishing the space with landscape timbers. It was an all-afternoon affair, and indescribably easier than trying to do all that by myself!

The sky was cloudless, and the sun was warm. We put a canvas and an umbrella in the yard for the babies, while the adults reveled in the warm sunshine and cooling breeze. And between the four adults (the babies didn't help much!), we got a lot done. It was not all manual labor, although much of it was. I also needed to determine what I was planting where, and how much space it would need. It took three of us to figure out the soaker-hose system and get it laid out along the garden. The give and take, the sharing of tasks, the planning and doing—it was like a garden in bloom!

Not only was it a lovely afternoon, but now my garden is ready for the summer plants.

I am excited by my waiting garden; there is joy in the anticipation of what is coming. My husband used to say that the anticipation of an event was every bit as enjoyable as the actual event: birthday, holiday, vacation.

Anticipation is born of a forward focus; I am living in the here and now, but I am thinking about and planning for the future.

> I consider that the sufferings of this present time are not worth comparing with the glory about to be revealed to us. (Romans 8:18)

Paul was living in a cell in Rome, but he was thinking about and planning for heaven.

Unlike heaven, of course, with my garden, there is the chance that my anticipation will lead to disappointment instead of fruition. But I don't think about that as I survey my prepared garden. The space is ready for peppers, tomato plants, and cucumber vines.

God has gifted me with an intrinsic joy in doing something now that will bear fruit only later. Matthew Sleeth, in *Reforesting Faith*, says this is the beauty of planting trees; you are planting them for future generations. My garden plants will reach fruition much sooner than a tree, but it is not immediate. I am engaging in an act of faith, taking action now in anticipatory joy of future results.

So the garden is ready. Soon the plants will go into the ground.

> Be glad and rejoice forever in what I am creating; for I am about to create Jerusalem as a joy, and its people as a delight. (Isaiah 65:18)

I am grateful that I had the time to prepare the garden. I am especially grateful that God made what would have been a chore for me into an enjoyable time with family.

What a blessing that God is creating something in this world, in our lives. What joy there is in anticipating His new world.

> The one who testifies to these things says, "Surely I am coming soon." Amen. Come, Lord Jesus. (Revelation 22:20)

Starter Plants

As I look to my left, a tangle of tall and aging sugar snaps greets me, scattered and messy. Weeds grow in and among the plants. It's a messy garden.

To my right, my summer garden is neat and orderly. Why? Because someone else has grown these tomatoes, cucumbers, and peppers from seed—all I need to do is transplant them into my garden. What a gift!

> From the bed where it was planted it was transplanted to good soil by abundant waters, so that it might produce branches and bear fruit and become a noble vine. (Ezekiel 17:8)

My spiritual journey can be scattered and messy, a tangle of confusing and conflicting thoughts. Christians have shared their growth with me, so all I need to do is transplant it into my life.

As I plant one tomato plant, I give thanks to God for Billy Graham, C. S. Lewis, and Charles Stanley, who started my growth. With the second, I give thanks for John Stott and Lee Strobel, who strengthened my faith with sound reasoning. With the third plant, I thank God for Henri Nouwen and Thomas Merton, who taught me quiet. With each successive plant, I thank the Lord for Martin Luther, John Calvin, St. Augustine, Karl Barth, N. T. Wright— these tremendous people of faith who have given me such a head start on my faith journey.

As I lower my cucumber seedlings into the ground, I remember the lessons of faith under fire taught by Richard Wurmbrand, Dietrich Bonhoeffer, Bob Fu, Foxe's Book of Martyrs. Could these hardy cucumbers withstand such persecution? Could I?

With the peppers, I give thanks for Bible teachers; people like

Eugene Peterson, Priscilla Shirer, Max Lucado, Ann Voskamp, and all those who have brought the Word to my living room.

These gifted thinkers, writers, and teachers have provided me with starter plants, seedlings for my garden. What a wonderful thing it is that God can plant their thoughts in my life and let them grow.

> Hold to the standard of sound teaching that you have heard from me, in the faith and love that are in Christ Jesus. (2 Timothy 1:13)

Now these plants are my responsibility. I need to ensure they have what they need—good soil, abundant water, and protected space to grow.

As wonderful as these plants are, and so much better than my attempts at growing from seed, it is not enough to stick them in the ground and ignore them. I need to let them take root and grow. Plants grow in two directions: unseen, they search out every hidden place underground; above ground, they spread their branches and produce fruit. I need to let the wisdom of those who have gone before do the same. I need to let the Word of God do the same.

> But as for you, continue in what you have learned and firmly believed, knowing from whom you learned it, and how from childhood you have known the scared writings that are able to instruct you for salvation through faith in Christ Jesus. (2 Timothy 3:14–15)

Today, I am grateful for everyone whose skill and expertise have grown these plants, transported these plants, and made these plants available to me. I am grateful that my garden stands a better chance of being successful because I have started with healthy plants. Let's get growing!

Roots

I gently squeeze the container around the starter plant and free the plant carefully from its constraints. In my hand, covered in dirt and grime, and looking like something from a horror flick, the thin roots wrap around each other and mass together.

These roots freed from the container seem fragile. They are precious. What happens with them will determine what happens to the plant. I know roots can be strong and immense, reach across the yard, wrap around underground pipes, and break up sidewalks and streets. But these roots, new as they are, are delicate.

This is the only time I get to see them. They are not pretty. But they are critical to the production of fruit. Without a healthy root system, the plant won't grow and bear fruit. Appearances can be so deceiving. Without the "ugly" root, the pretty flower never blooms.

> The members of the body that seem to be weaker are indispensable, and those members of the body that we think less honorable we cloth with greater honor. (1 Corinthians 12:22)

Once I have carefully planted my starter plants, there is a period of unseen activity. Nothing changes on the surface, but the roots are spreading out, reaching deeper, finding water and nutrients, and establishing themselves. Have you ever heard something very inspiring that seemed to rumble around in your head for weeks on end before it ever produced any visible change in your life? That is the Word taking root.

Letting God's Word take root is an important step to bearing the fruit He wants. I need to be like Mary and "ponder these things in my heart" (Luke 2:19). Too often, I jump to show off the new thing I have learned, without allowing it the time to develop properly.

I tried for a while to "give to everyone who begs from you" (Matthew 5:42)—exhausting and impractical. My dollar bills here and there accomplished little and put me on every call list in the nation. I had to slow down and let that verse take root. I sensed God was telling me to give based more on others' needs than my preferences for charities. My giving became less corporate and more personal. God has used the fruit He produced to answer some very specific needs. I just needed to give His Word time to grow roots.

> The ones on the rock are those who, when they hear the word, receive it with joy. But these have no root; they believe for a while and in a time of testing fall away. (Luke 8:13)

And just like the roots themselves, sometimes the root-growing process is not glamorous. There can be some ugly battles underground between those roots and the dirt that was there. I need to do my part to help them grow. Give them time, water them regularly, protect them from predators. For me, that means spending time quietly thinking about what is growing, what it may look like in maturity, what hidden hard places are limiting its growth, and perhaps even offering an "ugly cry" or two to water it.

There may even be a period of root shock when the plant seems to regress once you've transplanted it. The new life, the new idea, is taking a little time to adjust to its new environment. I need patience—with the plant, with nature, with myself, with others—because once the root establishes itself, the plant starts growing and wonderful fruit results.

> As you therefore have received Christ Jesus the Lord, continue to live your lives in him, rooted and built up in him and established in the faith, just as you were taught, abounding in thanksgiving. (Colossians 2:6–7)

You have planted a new garden. Let the starter plants take root. Fruit is on the horizon.

Water

Many gardening practices improve my garden's chances of success but aren't essential to the plants. Water is essential. Without water, the plants will perish.

Many Christian practices improve my relationship with God but aren't essential. Prayer is essential. Without prayer, without conversation with God, the relationship will perish.

In the spring in Tennessee, I don't need to worry about watering my garden much; it rains a lot. Nature (God) provides the water with no effort on my part. Sometimes in my life, prayer arises with no effort or thought on my part. Prayer can be a natural outpouring of gratitude, awe, need, or concern. I think, ideally, this is the way it should be. I think, in the kingdom of God, this is how it is.

> Rejoice always, pray without ceasing, give thanks in all circumstances; for this is the will of God in Christ Jesus for you. (1 Thessalonians 5:16–18)

But I'm not there yet. I need to be intentional about watering my garden, and I need to be intentional about prayer.

After Nick's cancer diagnosis, we went to the ocean several times a year, often for a week or two. Some of these trips occurred as the garden was growing, so we needed an automated watering system. He buried a pipeline to the spigot, attached it to a soaker hose spread throughout the garden, and installed a timer. When we were gone, the timer would turn on the hose every evening and water the garden.

Many times, our prayer lives are similar; there is an automatic nature to them. We pray at meals, before we go to bed, at Sunday worship, before and after Bible studies and church meetings. If the water is flowing and the prayer is sincere, this is a wonderful way to ensure our garden's survival.

But if my schedule is flexible and I will be in town, I prefer to water by hand. There's something about standing face to face with plants, gauging the amount of water each plant needs, observing the fresh growth and the weeds. It's more personal somehow, more intimate. I can wash off the bird droppings and the dust with a light mist.

And if I have not overscheduled myself and my mind is not elsewhere, this is how I like to pray. Set aside a time during the day to stand (sit or kneel) face to face with God, gauging my needs and His desires, observing my fresh growth and my weeds. It's more personal somehow, more intimate. I can ask for and receive forgiveness, gently given by one who knows exactly what I need.

What matters is that I pray. The manner, the situation, the impetus—none of that is as important as the actual heartfelt act of prayer.

> Devote yourselves to prayer, keeping alert in it with thanksgiving. (Colossians 4:2)

Even the words don't matter.

> Likewise the Spirit helps us in our weakness; for we do not know how to pray as we ought, but that very Spirit himself intercedes with sighs too deep for words. (Romans 8:26)

Keep the water flowing dear friends; keep praying.

Support

As I walk along the garden in the mornings, I see new growth. How proud I am of these little plants that are growing bigger and stronger every day! They stretch out their arms and reach for the sun. I know I had little to do with this. God is growing these plants, and it is marvelous in my sight!

I do have a role to play as they grow, however. I need to keep the branches resting on the supports.

Ever so gently, I lift the growing branches and rest them on the provided structure, the tomato cages. Metal uprights, braced by layers of rings and firmly planted in the soil, the cages help the plants bear the weight of emerging fruit.

Some fruits, like winter squash, pumpkins, and watermelon, have thick rinds that protect the yummy goodness from their surroundings, but tomatoes, cucumbers, and peppers do not. Their thinner skins would be pierced by the mulch and bruised by the ground. They need structure to lean on, structure to support them.

> Therefore, encourage one another and build up each other, as indeed you are doing. (1 Thessalonians 5:11)

My circle of Christian friends, my church, my Bible study groups—these are the structures in my life that support my growth. Without them, I have no doubt that I would be lying on the ground, rotting.

Most of us do not have thick enough skins to go through life without support or without structure. We need solid, sturdy support from upright people, braced by layers of faith and firmly planted in God's Word.

And we need to be that support for others as well. All of us, at one time or another, need one another. Even Moses needed the help of others to fulfill God's will.

> Whenever Moses held up his hand, Israel prevailed; and whenever he lowered his hand, Amalek prevailed. But Moses' hands grew weary; so they took a stone and put it under him, and he sat on it. Aaron and Hur held up his hands, one on one side, and the other on the other side; so his hands were steady until the sun set. (Exodus 17:11–12)

And do you know why these fine fellows knew Moses needed help? Because they were there with him.

If I do not go out and check on my plants daily, I may not notice their need for support until it is too late to help them. If I am not available to my friends, then I may never know they need assistance. If I do not alert my friends to my need for help, I may risk losing my own fruit.

> It will not be so among you; but whoever wishes to be great among you must be your servant, and whoever wishes to be first among you must be your slave; just as the Son of Man came not to be served, but to serve, and to give his life as a ransom for many. (Matthew 20:26–28)

Sometimes it can be humbling to ask for help; sometimes it can be demanding to provide it. But God calls us to humble ourselves (Luke 14:11) and look to the interests of others (Philippians 2:4).

All in the name of bearing fruit for the kingdom. If our goal is fruit, then whatever it takes to support its growth is not humiliating or a burden. Then we will share in the joy of seeing those growing plants bear wonderful, delicious fruit.

> This is the Lord's doing; it is marvelous in our eyes. (Psalm 118:23)

June

I take a deep breath and inhale the warmth, the cut grass, the scent of honeysuckle. I let the sun warm my face, my shoulders, and my back.

June is a special time in the garden. It is not time to plant or time to harvest. The summer plants have established themselves; the fence is secure; the sugar snaps are past their prime. I go out to the garden without tools and return without ripe fruit. But I do not return empty-handed. There is serenity in the slowness of June in the garden.

I am watching my plants grow. Daily, I tuck the growing tomato branches inside their cages, pick a few weeds that have burst through the barrier cloth, and check the moisture of the soil and water if needed. Mostly, I talk to the plants. Yes, I am that wacky old lady who talks to her plants.

Science has confirmed that talking to your plants encourages them to grow. I used to think that was just because we were expelling carbon dioxide, which the plants like to take in, but then I learned plants like harmonic music as well. Who knew plants could hear?

It turns out that trees, and probably most plants, make thousands of decisions throughout their lives, the complexities of which rival human decision-making. There is even a movement to declare trees as sentient beings. It is difficult for me to see my pepper plants are sentient beings, but they are certainly living things.

And all living things thrive on encouragement, praise, and support. "Look at those new leaves, cucumber! Good job! Let me lift your branch up for you, sweet tomato. That fruit will get heavy! That little pepper is getting so big! Way to go!"

> And we urge you, beloved, to admonish the idlers, encourage the fainthearted, help the weak, be patient with all of them. (1 Thessalonians 5:14)

That is really all I can do right now—encourage my plants. These plants will bear fruit when it is their time to bear fruit; that fruit will ripen when it ripens. Since I have no control over those things, I choose to enjoy, savor even, this time of tranquility.

I can feel the morning sun on my face and feel the breeze cooling my neck. When I lift the tomato branches, their aroma fills my nose to the point I can taste it. When I pull a weed, soft soil brings up the scents of the earth; an earthworm scoots for cover. As I stand and face the sky, I take a deep breath and feel connected to all of God's creation.

> The earth is the Lord's and all that is in it, the world and those that live in it. (Psalm 24:1)

With the industrial revolution, the move to cities, electricity, and cars, we have become increasingly indoor people. Unless we go to a farmers market, we are several steps removed from the source of our food. We no longer walk to work; few of us work outside or play outside. Culturally, we have lost our connection to the earth, but there is grassroots effort to rectify that (pun intended).

For me, the garden, and specifically the garden in June, helps me reestablish that connection.

In June, I can just go out and *be* in the garden. While I talk to my plants, they sometimes seem to talk to me, telling me about God and His creation, and teaching me what they have learned over millennia. Often, I just stand or sit with them.

> Be still and know that I am God! I am exalted among the nations, I am exalted in the earth. (Psalm 46:10)

I encourage you to go outside today. Look for a flower in bloom or a weed overcoming its concrete prison. Sit under a tree or admire its leaves. Breathe in the scent of earth or cut grass or roses. Feel the sun and the breeze and the blades of some petal nearby. The earth exalts God. Let's take a moment today to join in that exultation.

Corralling Cucumbers

The leaves push through the fence, the branches stretch out into the yard; green tendrils search for some new land to conquer. The cucumbers are at it again!

Cucumbers, like all their squash cousins, are rambunctious, exuberant, enthusiastic plants. They will grow to fill whatever space you have provided and then grow some more. Fences are mere obstacles easily overcome. These eager plants grow through my fences and over the boundaries I place in their way.

When I walk my garden every day, I must put the cucumbers' vines back inside the fence. I need to be just as enthusiastic as they are.

I love their enthusiasm. I can relate. I often feel like I am on the verge of being out of control, like I am testing the boundaries and going outside the fence. I am grateful that God sends His Spirit to corral my exuberance.

> When the Spirit of truth comes, he will guide you into all the truth. (John 16:13)

My ministers, my Christian friends, the Bible—all help me stay inside the fence, help me stay in the right relationship, help my wandering thoughts to return to God and Jesus.

> All scripture is inspired by God and is useful for teaching, for reproof, for correction and for training in righteousness. (2 Timothy 3:16)

And you know what? This rambunctious, exuberant, enthusiastic attitude is exactly what makes cucumbers and their squash cousins such prolific producers of fruit. They have no fear, no timidity, no apparent caution. They just keep growing until a stronger hand moves them back inside the fence.

I think God likes enthusiasm.

> Do not lag in zeal, be ardent in spirit, serve the Lord.
> (Romans 12:11)

In John's Revelation, only the church of Laodicea receives no praise.

> So, because you are lukewarm, and neither cold nor hot, I am about to spit you out of my mouth.
> (Revelation 3:16)

So grow with abandon, dear cucumbers! I will corral and correct your growth, just as God corrals and corrects mine. I hope that my enthusiasm makes God smile as much as the cucumbers' enthusiasm makes me smile.

I pray I can be enthusiastic about serving the Lord, about growing in my faith, about becoming all that God has planned for me to be, like my cucumbers.

Perhaps you relate more to the prized tomato plant or the independent pepper plants, even perhaps the fragile sugar snap. Praise God that he grows all plants in His garden. Praise God that He cares for each plant in the manner best suited to its specific needs. Please know that He values, grows, and cares for each of you as well.

> God said, "See, I have given you every plant yielding seed that is upon the face of all the earth, and every tree with seed in its fruit; you shall have them for food. (Genesis 1:29)

Keep growing, my friend!

Keep Out!

The robin sits on the framework of my garden and tilts his head. I can almost hear him: "Are those tomatoes ripe enough for me to peck?" A squirrel barks at me from the nearby tree, claiming the tomatoes as his own. I regret to inform you, friend robin and mister squirrel, these tomatoes are not for you!

Every summer I go through the ridiculously laborious task of putting up bird netting. After several summers of losing our tomatoes to the birds, Nick erected a metal pole frame over which we could lay the netting. The netting is almost invisible and catches on everything, even grass. The effort of unfolding and unrolling the netting and draping it over the metal poles, which are taller than me, tests my patience.

It's not something I can do by myself.

Do I really need to go to all this effort? Yes! I have gardened for thirty years and lost countless tomatoes to birds and squirrels. What a waste to pour so much time and effort into growing them, only to lose out at the end and not be able to reap the benefits.

Am I willing to exert that effort to protect my spiritual fruit from predators who aim to destroy it?

> For our struggle is not against enemies of blood and flesh, but ... against the spiritual forces of evil in the heavenly places. Therefore, take up the whole armor of God, so that you may be able to ... stand firm. (Ephesians 6:12–13)

Because just as red tomatoes stand out against green leaves, your spiritual fruit will stand out against the background of worldly living. If you are loving when you have every right to be angry, if you are gentle when many would use force, if you are peaceful in a time of unrest, others will notice. Some will admire you and rejoice, but others will take advantage of you, apply more pressure, and maybe even make you a target.

To make sure that my fruit continues to ripen unscarred and protected from those who would destroy it, I need to shield it with bird netting. I need to erect a barrier between my fruit, the evidence of the Holy Spirit in my life, and the world around me, a barrier that is almost invisible but keeps the fruit intact.

> Do not be conformed to this world, but be transformed by the renewing of your minds, so that you may discern what is the will of God—what is good and acceptable and perfect. (Romans 12:2)

Like putting up bird netting, renewing our minds is not a simple task. It can be time-consuming and frustrating. It catches on our emotions and knee-jerk reactions. We, I often fall far short of what is good or acceptable, much less perfect.

But don't give up. Keep at the task, because that layer of protection is the only way the fruit can ripen undisturbed.

> Now, discipline always seems painful rather than pleasant at the time, but later it yields the peaceful fruit of righteousness. (Hebrews 12:11)

It's not something I can do by myself.

I need my church. I need my Christian friends. I need the Holy Spirit—after all, it's His fruit that's growing!

> Pray in the Spirit at all times in every prayer and supplication. (Ephesians 6:18)

How sad it would be to lose what fruit God has grown in me because I did not make the effort to protect it. So while social expectation may tilt its head at me, wondering if I'll play its game, and worldly ways may bark at me, trying to claim my affections, I will boldly inform them to keep out of my garden.

> And the peace of God, which surpasses all understanding, will guard your hearts and your minds in Christ Jesus. (Philippians 4:7)

An Unwelcome Visitor

I had an unwelcome visitor in my garden this morning, lured in by the unmowed grasses and water-fed weeds. No bigger than a chipmunk, the baby bunny was more interested in my weeds than my tomatoes. Perhaps he wanted to nibble on the companion flowers, supposedly a repellent for rodents, perhaps not so much for rabbits.

My presence sent him into a panic, racing back and forth along the fence, looking desperately for an exit point. I would not have hurt the bunny, but he didn't know that. I am much bigger and stronger than he is, so I could have hurt him; I could have killed him. Instead, I stopped to get a picture and let him catch his breath. Then I lifted an edge of the fencing and gave him a way out. I wanted him out of my garden. Eventually, he found his exit and fled to the safety of the hedgerow.

> Just then there was in their synagogue a man with an unclean spirit, and he cried out, "What have you to do with us, Jesus of Nazareth? Have you come to destroy us? I know who you are, the Holy One of God." But Jesus rebuked him saying, "Be silent, and come out of him!" (Mark 1:24–25)

Not all predators are satanic evils threatening our existence. Some are cute little bunnies looking for a new place to dine. I thought about letting the bunny stay. If I had, he probably would have died from heart failure. My daily presence would make the garden a less enjoyable place for the bunny.

Perhaps the Holy Spirit's presence in our lives makes us a less enjoyable place for ungodly forces to visit.

Perhaps the appearance of the Holy Spirit sends our ungodly thoughts into a panic, racing back and forth along the fence, looking desperately for an exit point. Maybe if we invited the Holy Spirit into our lives daily, the ungodly forces would either die from heart failure or leave us for friendlier and safer spaces.

Once the bunny was gone from the garden, I examined the fence and netting all around the tomatoes. How had he gained entry? What space had I left unguarded? What gap had he wiggled through?

When I discover unwelcome, ungodly thoughts running rampant in my mind, the Holy Spirit can drive them out, but I need to examine my life. Where did these thoughts come from? How did they get in? Was it that trashy movie I watched? Or that godless and depressing book?

I need to find the gap because if that cute little bunny can get inside, tomato-stealing chipmunks and squirrels can as well. If little ungodly thoughts find an easy residence in my mind, larger, more dangerous thoughts can as well.

> Be on guard so that your hearts are not weighed down with dissipation and drunkenness and the worries of this life. (Luke 21:34)

When I go out tomorrow to check on the garden, I will check carefully for evidence of the bunny's return. If he has been back, I will recheck the fencing. Lesson learned, I hope.

Have I learned this lesson in my life? How much of my peace and patience and joy and love of others have I lost to unwelcome visitors like worry, insecurity, fear, and selfishness?

God is big and scary to these petty concerns, much bigger and stronger than these unwelcome visitors. His presence will send them racing for an exit from my life. His continued presence will keep them out.

> He commands even the unclean spirits, and they obey Him. (Mark 1:27)

Weeds

Despite having tilled my garden space and put down weed-barrier cloth, there are still weeds in my garden. Ugh, I wish there weren't.

Weeds sap water and nutrients away from my vegetable plants. Weeds entangle my young plants and pull them to the ground.

Weeds are unavoidable. The garden is in the yard, so of course, the yard creeps into the garden space. Weeding is without a doubt my least favorite part of gardening, but I need to do it, because the weeds will hinder my plants' growth.

Jesus compared weeds to the cares and pleasures of life.

> As for what fell among the thorns, these are the ones who hear; but as they go on their way, they are choked by the cares and riches and pleasures of life, and their fruit does not mature. (Luke 8:14)

I live in the world, so of course, the cares and pleasures of the world creep into my relationship with God, but I need to weed them out before they sap my resources, hinder my growth, choke out the Spirit, and pull me to the ground.

> Therefore, since we are surrounded by so great a cloud of witnesses, let us also lay aside every weight and the sin that clings so closely. (Hebrews 12:1)

The cares and pleasures of the world are not bad things, as weeds are not bad things. In fact, by definition, weeds are just plants growing where you don't want them to grow. Dandelions provide many benefits for the soil and for humans, but I don't want them in my garden.

The best advice is to weed daily. Every time I go out to the garden, I look for weeds and pull a few. Normally, these are the weeds that are encroaching on the plants or are big and visible. I try to pull these before they become too well established and cause problems.

Ideally, this would keep my garden weed-free, but it doesn't. To really rid my garden of weeds, I need to set aside more time than my morning walk-through allows. To really examine those things that are hindering my spiritual growth and weed them out of my life may take more time than my morning devotional allows. I may need to set aside a time for just this purpose and ask God to show me the weeds.

> Search me, O God, and know my heart; test me and know my thoughts. See if there is any wicked way in me, and lead me in the way everlasting. (Psalm 139:23–24)

Perhaps I don't like to weed because I rather like weeds. I love to see an abandoned field covered in wildflowers. I love the dainty white and purple and yellow blossoms throughout my yard before the mowers cut them down. That dandelion pushing through the concrete inspires me. God has brought beauty to the world in the most unlikely places—what an amazing gift! Just so, God has given us earthly pleasures like good food and wine and fellowship. They all have their place.

Weeding our spiritual garden does not mean we are to become puritanical in our elimination of earthly joys, but we are to keep them in their proper place and keep them from becoming our focus.

> Therefore do not worry, saying, "What will we eat?" or "What will we drink?" or "What will we wear?" For it is the gentiles who strive for all these things; and indeed your heavenly Father knows that you need all these things. But strive first for the kingdom of God

and his righteousness, and all these things will be given to you as well. (Matthew 6:31–33)

And you know what? There is beauty in a weed-free garden. With help, I cleared my tomatoes and peppers of weeds. My cucumbers are next. I know the weeds will creep back, mandating my continued vigilance, but there is a weightlessness, a sense of relief, an optimism that forces a smile upon my face as I look at my weed-free garden space. Joy—a fruit of the Spirit.

Waiting

I don't like to wait. I don't even like to shop. If I need something, I get it. No reason to waste time thinking about it forever.

But that doesn't work in the garden.

In the garden, I must wait. I must wait for the plants to grow. I must wait for the fruit to appear. I must wait for the fruit to ripen. No amount of wishing or impatience on my part changes that.

Every day, I walk in the garden. I check on the growth, make sure they have enough water, correct and support the growth as needed, watch, and wait. And wait.

The tomatoes are there. They are large and green. And still green.

Waiting—it's possibly the hardest thing to do, especially for us in the here and now. If we lived in the millennia before digital communications, we would have to wait for information to arrive. If we lived in a time of austerity, we would have to wait until something was available that we could afford. As it is, we live in a world besotted with self-determination, going for it, instant communication, immediate gratification, easy credit, and overabundance.

Maybe waiting is difficult for you as well.

> Wait for the Lord; be strong, and let your heart take courage; wait for the Lord! (Psalm 27:14)

If you read the Old Testament, waiting was never something that people found easy. Sarah couldn't wait for Isaac's birth, but had her servant conceive Ishmael; their descendants are still fighting. The Hebrews in the desert couldn't wait for Moses to return, so they created a molten calf to lead them. There are many instances of God asking His people to wait, and many instances of God's people complaining about having to wait.

> How long, O Lord? (Psalm 13:1, also Psalm 119:84, Habakkuk 1:2, Psalm 89:46)

But in a garden, you must wait. Work while you wait, but wait. There is no point in complaining or fretting or getting anxious about how long it is taking the plant to mature. It just takes time. I just have to wait.

> Do not worry about anything, but in everything by prayer and supplication with thanksgiving let your requests be made known to God. (Philippians 4:6)

What a lesson for life. Some things take time.

It takes time for those green tomatoes to turn red. Sometimes it takes time for me to forgive someone. It has taken a long time for me to stay calm when someone cuts in front of me. It may take time before God fulfills His promise to you. In the meantime, God calls us to have faith and wait.

> Be patient, therefore, beloved, until the coming of the Lord. The farmer waits for the precious crop from the earth, being patient with it until it receives the early and the late rains. You also must be patient. Strengthen your hearts, for the coming of the Lord is near. (James 5:7–8)

So be patient. Wait on the Lord. He is at work, even if we can't see it. Have faith. Fear not. Fret not. When the time is right, the plant will grow and bear fruit. When the time is right, the fruit will be ready.

And the good news is, since patience is a fruit of the Spirit, your ability to wait for God to accomplish His plans is evidence of His fruit ripening in your life.

Take a deep breath, my friend, and enjoy your summer.

Robbed

I had my first tomato sandwich yesterday—delicious! There were several more tomatoes on the vine. I was so looking forward to picking, eating, and sharing them.

This morning, they are all gone. Every one of them—robbed. My guess is that whatever took them got under the bird netting and up and over the fence, probably a squirrel.

Fortunately, I have planted indeterminate tomatoes, and I think I will get new blossoms, new tomatoes. For now, the problem is preventing the predators from returning. I need to secure the netting and check my fence for openings. I need to search my garden for how the squirrel got in and correct the problem.

What I don't need to do is get all upset about the lost tomatoes. It is in the squirrel's nature to test any obstacles in its way. And the purpose of a test is to show us what we have mastered and where we need to improve. My netting is protecting the garden from the birds but needs some work to withstand the squirrels.

> Examine yourselves to see whether you are living in faith. Test yourselves. Do you not realize that Jesus Christ is in you?—unless, indeed, you fail to meet the test! (2 Corinthians 13:5)

I had a dustup with a friend. It has exposed a gap in my spiritual netting. I am too busy justifying my actions to feel remorse, too offended to feel compassion, and too self-righteous to humble myself. I am angry. So is she. The thief came in the night and robbed me of the fruit of the Spirit. What I need to do is examine myself and discover how I let that happen. Where are the gaps in the fence, the open spaces in the netting? How was I so easily robbed? I need to correct the problem.

> Create in me a clean heart, O God, and put a new and
> right spirit within me. (Psalm 51:10)

What I don't need to do is dwell on the problem, stress over it, and fixate on it. More important than the lost tomatoes is the realization that I need to fix my netting. More important than the dustup is the realization that I need to realign myself with God.

I have trouble letting the past go. It is a challenge to not relive the mistakes I've made, the wounds I have inflicted, the wounds inflicted upon me. Dwelling on past hurts can easily consume my day. But the past does not need to determine who I am—even the recent past. Whatever I did wrong yesterday, and I am sure there was plenty, does not mandate what my actions today will be.

Today is a new day.

I will water my garden and try again to protect it from robbers and thieves.

> The thief comes only to steal and kill and destroy.
> I have come that they may have life and have it
> abundantly. (John 10:10)

God has given me this new day and the promise of new blossoms. God has shown me I cannot manifest His fruit by my own abilities. I need God, and I need to be vigilant against my baser self or evil forces robbing me of the Spirit's fruit.

Fortunately, God has also given me the ability to do just that.

> But to all who received him, who believed in his name,
> he gave power to become children of God. (John 1:12)

I will not let the tomato robber end my garden. I will not let the peace robber end my spiritual journey. These are setbacks and disappointments; these are tests I have failed. But God has given me faith and hope and love. Thank You, Lord!

Go in peace, dear friend, go in the peace of God.

Heat of the Summer

We had record heat this summer, weeks of temperatures in the upper nineties. My pepper plants love it. I can't remember the last time I had peppers in late June, although it was probably ten years ago when we had a similar early heat wave. Usually, I have to wait until late July.

One year, we had to wait until August. Heat is the main stressor for most plants. Although stressing the plant artificially was an option, we waited; it was bound to get hot at some point. And of course, it did.

As unpredictable as the weather can be year-to-year, month-to-month, or day-to-day, we know there will be periods of unseasonable temperatures when it is too hot or too cold. There will be excessive rainfall and periods of drought. There will be storms. We just don't know when.

As humans, we strive to insulate ourselves from these unpleasant situations. We have built protective homes, installed heating and A/C units to moderate the temperature, and comfortable beds and chairs. But my garden is not that protected. My plants are dealing with the weather head-on.

And the peppers are thriving.

> My brothers and sisters, whenever you face trials of any kind, consider it nothing but joy, because you know that the testing of your faith produces endurance; and let endurance have its full effect, so that you may be mature and complete, lacking in nothing. (James 1:2–4)

Maybe we only produce fruit when we are stressed or when we are facing trials.

And who knows if my pepper plants are really loving this heat?

They may not enjoy the stressful situation that encourages their fruit production. They may even resent being in such a situation. But their fruit is a beautiful thing.

> Knowing that suffering produces endurance, and endurance produces character, and character produces hope, and hope does not disappoint us. (Romans 5:3–5)

Do I love being in situations that make me bear fruit? Can I show patience if I am never frustrated? Am I showing love and kindness if I only spend time with people I like? Will I bear the fruit of gentleness if nothing angers me?

Maybe we, like the plants, need stress, need the heat of the summer to bear our fruit.

Maybe that heat reveals if we are bearing the fruit of the Spirit or the fruit of our own selfish desires.

How am I reacting to the stress, to the heat? Because this has already been an extremely hot summer. This has already been an incredibly stressful summer, and not only for my garden.

Just turn on the news for fifteen minutes.

Am I bearing fruit? Am I bearing the Spirit's fruit? Are you?

As a gardener, I look forward to the heat of the summer. The heat makes the plants produce the fruit I want.

I admit I rarely look forward to heat and stress in my life. I rarely consider it joy. And yet if it makes me produce that fruit, isn't it a good thing?

Perhaps I will learn to welcome situations that cause me to bear fruit, as I welcome the heat of summer.

My prayer is that you and I will bear much holy fruit this summer.

Trial and Error

I tried something new in my garden this year—Ruby Kisses.

According to the seed catalog, coreopsis, aka Ruby Kiss, is one of the most squirrel-repellent flowers available. After losing most of my tomatoes to squirrels and chipmunks last year, I was in for adding these lovely-sounding plants to my garden.

The problems started when the seed packet arrived. For some reason I can't recall now, I started these flowers in trays on my kitchen table. Surely, I did not read that I should start these flowers this way—what a disaster! After purchasing seed trays and potting soil, I dutifully surrendered my kitchen table to the process. Soon, towels also covered my table, to protect it from the excess or errant water and ever-present dirt. Most of the seeds didn't come up, but little green sprouts crowded a few of the pots. So I got some larger pots, biodegradable ones that I could put right in the soil when the time came. I only killed about half the plants in the transplanting process.

By the time I was ready to plant my tomatoes, I had about eight two-inch-tall plants to add to my garden—definitely not worth the effort and mess. I bought some marigolds when I bought the tomatoes. Although not as effective, according to Google, they were pretty and available and mostly grown.

Just for kicks, I also planted my struggling Ruby Kiss seedlings among the tomatoes and marigolds. I mean, why not?

Now it's hard to tell if I am growing tomatoes or wildflowers. The Ruby Kisses have taken over the garden! What a mess!

The beauty of a garden is that I now know not to pursue Ruby Kisses in the future.

> If we confess our sins, he who is faithful and just will forgive us our sins and cleanse us from all unrighteousness. (1 John 1:9)

Sometimes, I have to learn things the hard way, by trial and error.

You know what else is not good for my garden? Resentment. I had to learn that one the hard way too. I have nurtured resentment along, feeling it was justified; transplanted it into bigger pots like my family and friends; and spilled dirt all over my kitchen table. What a mess. Just have to dig that up and never plant it again.

Condescension is like Ruby Kisses as well. I sense it will protect me, but soon it overshadows my fruit. When others look at my garden, is that all they see? Maybe a tomato is hidden in there somewhere?

The beauty of life, and particularly life with Christ, is that we get a new garden every day.

> Search me, O God, and know my heart; test me and know my thoughts. See if there is any wicked way in me and lead me in the way everlasting. (Psalm 139:23–24)

Perhaps, instead of trying to justify why I am growing Ruby Kisses in my garden, I should be grateful for the lesson learned. Instead of feeling guilty about my errors, I should simply uproot the plant and move forward, and see this as a learning moment (a test?). Have I let sin grow in my life just as I have let Ruby Kisses grow in my garden?

What a gift that God allows us to try and fail. What a gift that God gives us the opportunity to try again, to have a redo, a makeup test. What a difference it would make if I could look at test results and see not where I failed, but where I could improve.

> Create in me a clean heart, O God, and put a new and right spirit within me. (Psalm 51:10)

God loves us. We do not need to have a perfect garden for Him to love us. He already does.

We do not need to ace a test; I think we never will this side of heaven. God wants what is best for us. He wants to grow joy and peace and love in our gardens and in our lives. If we mess up occasionally and plant some Ruby Kisses, He forgives us. I've learned my lesson. Thank You, Lord.

Garden Shoes

They sit by the back door expectantly, waiting for me to slip them on. Worn out, worn in, scuffed, muddy, and comfortable, these are my garden shoes. These shoes are as important to my garden as the fencing and the bird netting.

This morning, I slipped them on as I headed to the garden. The yard, covered in dew, strewn with grass clippings, muddy with yesterday's rain, riddled with thorny plants and industrious bees, can be a messy place. Inside my shoes, my feet are dry, clean, and safe.

Without these shoes dedicated to this less-than-glamorous role in life, either my feet would be in peril, or my fancier shoes would be.

Their appearance in no way diminishes their importance—quite the opposite. Their worn-out, worn-in, scruffy, muddy, comfortable countenance is what gives them value and makes them perfect for the role of garden shoe.

> But God has so arranged the body, giving the greater honor to the inferior member, that there may be no dissension within the body, but the members may have the same care for one another. (1 Corinthians 12:24–25)

Has God assigned you a less-than-glamorous role in life? Are you worn out, scruffy, and covered in yard debris? Do you feel like an inferior member? Haven't we all felt that way at some point?

Maybe your infant has just thrown up on your one clean shirt, or your mom has wandered down the street in her pajamas, looking for the dog that died three years ago. Maybe the dishes have piled up in the sink and the toilet backed up in the bathroom. Maybe your boss has trashed your work and told you to start again, again. Maybe your body has failed you, leaving only wishes with no option of action.

You have a very crucial role in the kingdom of God. You are every bit as much a part of God's garden as the ministers and the missionaries.

> In a large house there are utensils not only of gold and silver but also of wood and clay, some for special use, some for ordinary. (2 Timothy 2:20)

All are valuable. Could you imagine using your silver goblet to measure flour? The silver goblet may be shiny and precious and placed where all can see, but the plastic measuring cup is far more useful, more functional, more necessary, and more important to daily life.

I wouldn't wear my garden shoes to a ladies' luncheon, but I depend on them.

And Jesus tells us that God values the less-glamorous servants highly.

> Whoever wants to be first must be last of all and servant of all. (Mark 9:35, also Matthew 20:26, Luke 22:26)

Maybe in the tables-turned, topsy-turvy kingdom of heaven, God will give my garden shoes the place of honor.

Maybe in the tables-turned, topsy-turvy kingdom of heaven, God will give the parent, the caregiver, the housekeeper, the worker, and the invalid seats of honor.

> So the last will be first, and the first will be last. (Matthew 20:16, 19:30)

If you are feeling like a worn-out pair of garden shoes today, take heart. If we are following Jesus, He will give us the work He needs us to do, glamorous or not. His Spirit within us will make us "dedicated and useful to the owner of the house, ready for every good work" (2 Timothy 2:21).

My garden shoes wait patiently for me to slip them on. Just a little walk out to the garden, around and through it, then back inside. Job done, they rest. How happy these shoes make me, doing their little job so well. I do not see their age, their misshapen body, their dirty exterior covered in yard debris; I see their faithful, useful service.

> Well done, good and trustworthy slave; you have been trustworthy in a few things, I will put you in charge of many things; enter into the joy of your master. (Matthew 25:21)

Autumn Harvest

Autumn is a time of harvest when God ripens the fruit on mature plants, yielding a blessing for all. Autumn is when God shares His bounty with the world.

He put before them another parable: "The kingdom of heaven may be compared to someone who sowed good seed in his field; but while everybody was asleep, an enemy came and sowed weeds among the wheat, and then went away. So when the plants came up and bore grain, then the weeds appeared as well. And the slaves of the householder came and said to him, 'Master, did you not sow good seed in your field? Where, then, did these weeds come from?' He answered, 'An enemy has done this.' The slaves said to him, 'Then do you want us to go and gather them?' But he replied, 'No; for in gathering the weeds you would uproot the wheat along with them. Let both of them grow together until the harvest; and at harvest time I will tell the reapers, 'Collect the weeds first and bind them in bundles to be burned, but gather the wheat into my barn.'" (Matthew 13:24-30)

And His disciples approached Him, saying, "Explain to us the parable of the weeds of the field." He answered, "The one who sows the good seed is the Son of Man; the field is the world, and the good seed are the children of the kingdom; the weeds are the children of the evil one, and the enemy who sowed them is the devil; the harvest is the end of the age, and the reapers are the angels. Just as the weeds are collected up and burned with fire, so will it be at the end of the age. The Son of Man will send his angels, and they will collect out of his kingdom all causes of sin and all evildoers, and they will be thrown into the furnace of fire, where there will be weeping and gnashing of teeth. Then the righteous will shine like the sun in the kingdom of their Father. Let anyone with ears listen!" (Matthew 13:36-43)

True Beauty

The leaves are brown and curling, the branches droop. As the tomato and cucumber plants yield their fruit, their once-verdant leaves begin to fall. As the heavy fruit weighs down the branches, they hang over the supports, barely upright. The plant is putting all its energy into producing fruit, no longer concerned about its appearance.

Of course, it is every bit as beautiful to me as it was as a young plant. As excited as I was to see its growing green leaves, I am more excited to see its ripening fruit.

> Do not adorn yourselves outwardly ... rather, let your adornment be the inner self with the lasting beauty of a gentle and quiet spirit, which is very precious in God's sight. (1 Peter 3:3–4)

Perhaps this happens to us as we mature as Christians as well. As we focus more on deepening our relationship with God and encouraging the growth of His Spirit's fruit in our lives, we have fewer resources to give to our outward appearance. Perhaps at some point, being patient and kind becomes more important than the wrinkles on our face.

After all, I did not grow those tomatoes to be beautiful plants in my garden. I grew them to bear tomatoes.

I don't believe God put us in this place and time just to have people admire us. He put us here for a reason: to bear His fruit, to love one another, to further His kingdom.

> For we are what he has made us, created in Christ Jesus for good works, which God prepared beforehand to be our way of life. (Ephesians 2:10)

How beautiful we must be in God's eyes when we bear His fruit, when we do His will! This is why He created us, planted us in this place, and provided His food and water for us. Who cares if our leaves brown and wilt? Who cares if spots appear and our branches droop? The beauty of young things may encourage us to care for them, but true lasting beauty comes in maturity.

And how convenient this aging out of the garden occurs as social activities start, although that is no coincidence. The school year was set when we were a largely agrarian society.

School, football, volunteer work—all that could wait until the crops were in. So in the summer, I tend to my garden and swim in the lake. In the fall, I go to Bible studies and committee meetings and watch football. This rhythm is still very ingrained in us, even as we move to year-round school in our post-agrarian society.

When my kids were in school, Nick and I battled the push for year-round school. At some deep level, I appreciate that there are seasons for things. Not every day should look the same; not every month should mimic the month before. Maybe because I have a garden, I appreciate the cycle of growth, production, and rest. Nonstop sameness is a product of industrialization, out of sync with the natural flow created by God.

On a bigger scale, this rhythm and flow, this constant change, is part of our spiritual life as well. There are times of growth, times of production, and times of rest. Even as we honor God in everything we do (Colossians 3:17), we have seasons of study, seasons of service, and seasons of quiet communion with God.

And there is beauty in all of it. God sees it, even if others may not.

> For the Lord does not see as mortals see; they look on the outward appearance, but the Lord looks on the heart. (1 Samuel 16:7)

So when I look at these plants, I do not see the browning leaves but the beautiful fruit. When I look at my older Christian friends, I do not see the lines on their faces but the love in their eyes and the smiles on their lips. I pray we can be beautiful in every season.

Worth the Effort

What a decision I must make today—shall I have a tomato or a cucumber on my sandwich? Maybe both! Few things can compare to the incredible flavor of a homegrown tomato, topped with a little freshly cut basil. But the crisp sweetness of a cucumber just off the vine comes close.

The scent of basil on my hands decides for me—tomato it is.

I remember how much work it took getting the garden tilled and fenced. I remember sweating in the heat, my arms and back aching as I planted each little seedling. I gaze at the metal poles supporting the bird netting and remember Nick's labor to erect them.

Was it worth it? Yes!

> Therefore, my beloved, be steadfast, immovable, always excelling in the work of the Lord, because you know that in the Lord your labor is not in vain. (1 Corinthians 15:58)

I do not claim to excel in gardening or much of anything else, for that matter. But God has granted me the gift of persistence, a willingness to keep at it and see it through. Much of that comes from faith, a conviction that if I am doing what God is calling me to do and listening to His voice, my labor will not be in vain.

And walking in God's will can be labor. It can be physical labor, like the garden. It can be emotional labor, like forgiveness and reconciliation. You may become exhausted and sweaty. Sometimes it is easier to sleep in instead of going to church. Sometimes I would rather binge-watch mindless TV than make those phone calls or write those letters.

> Those who till their land will have plenty of food, but those who follow worthless pursuits have no sense. (Proverbs 12:11)

Then I look at these tomatoes and cucumbers. I know that this fruit was worth the effort.

The fruit of the Spirit is worth the effort as well. Knowing that God will grow gentleness and patience in my life is worth making time every morning to read His Word. His peace and joy are worth spending time every day in prayer, presenting my concerns and listening for His response.

> By contrast, the fruit of the Spirit is love, joy, peace, patience, kindness, generosity, faithfulness, gentleness, and self-control. (Galatians 5:22)

I want that fruit as much as I want these tomatoes and cucumbers—even if it takes effort on my part, even if giving the Spirit space to grow this fruit disrupts my plans or unsettles my easy way of life. I may need to uproot some weeds and plant some good seeds. It may be hard. But the harvest is worth the effort.

When I feel kindness growing where once criticism flourished, I know being in His presence was worth the effort. When I can react in gentleness instead of anger, I am looking at His fruit in my life. When helping someone in need brings me more joy than a rising bank balance, I know God is growing something eternal in my heart.

> O taste and see that the Lord is good. (Psalm 34:8)

What wonders of God's riches will I enjoy today?

Pick the Fruit

The cucumbers are ripe, the peppers have turned red, and the tomatoes are ready to eat.

I need to pick today. If I leave the cucumbers too long, they will turn sour and seedy. If I leave the tomatoes, they will split or get mushy. Even the peppers will rot if left too long.

Tomorrow, there will be more to pick. Because I planted indeterminate plants, this is happening over a period of weeks instead of all at the same time. As I pick, more ripen.

In fact, if I do not pick the ripe fruit, I delay the production of more fruit. Perhaps the plant only has so much energy to share, and it goes to the ripe fruit before it goes to the emerging fruit. In this sense, picking the fruit is a sort of pruning that allows for more resources to be sent to emerging fruit.

Pruning is the act of cutting back parts of a plant so that other parts can flourish. Much less important in backyard gardens than in a vineyard, pruning dead branches and deadheading flowers can still improve any crop. Perhaps picking the fruit accomplishes the same goal.

> Every branch that bears fruit he prunes to make it bear more fruit. (John 15:2)

Nick liked to think that it made the plant happy to know that we desired its fruit—that our picking the fruit encouraged the plant to produce more. And I want happy, fruit-producing plants.

After all, everyone likes to feel appreciated. We all want at least one other person to enjoy what we are producing, what we are putting into the world, and what we are gifting to the cosmos. And when others seem to appreciate our efforts, we are more likely to continue them.

> Therefore encourage one another and build up each other, as indeed you are doing. (1 Thessalonians 5:11)

Also, the fruit I grow in my garden, like the fruit the Spirit grows in my life, has a purpose. And it is not to sit on the vine and rot.

We may not know the purpose of what is growing in our lives. Like the tomato I give away, I may never know its end use.

But one thing I know. Every fruit has a purpose beyond its own existence.

Fruit propagates more plants and benefits every creature that partakes of it. That beautiful tomato does not exist to make the plant look pretty. And God does not give us joy and peace so that we can be joyful and peaceful in our home by ourselves.

God gives us His fruit to propagate His kingdom and benefit every creature on this earth. What a waste it would be to let it rot on the vine, to deny that fruit its larger purpose.

> "I was afraid, and I went and hid your talent in the ground. Here you have what is yours." But his master replied, "You wicked and lazy slave!" (Matthew 25:25–26)

So I am headed out to the garden to pick a cucumber or two, a couple of tomatoes, and maybe even a pepper. Maybe I'll have them as a salad or as a sandwich. They will provide me with vital nutrients to support me for another day.

And I will thank God for growing them in my garden. I thank Him for my yard, the sun, the rain, the fruit itself, and the ability to pick it, eat it, and share it.

Bad Fruit

When you buy starter plants, they are in trays that have labels at the end. The supplier marks each plant individually, but I don't always look at the individual labels—a recipe for disaster.

One year, we planted small, sweet peppers. We had a recipe for stuffing them with cheese and were eager to make a bunch. We bought two plants. But as they grew, one looked a little off, with slightly different-shaped leaves, a darker hue, and thinner peppers. Nick reasoned that he should try one before we stuffed them.

I still don't know what they were—ghost peppers, perhaps? His mouth on fire, tears streaming down his red face, stuffing bread into his mouth, Nick washed his face and hands and arms repeatedly.

With gloves, we packed all the harvested peppers in a bag, dug up the plant, and gave it all to a friend who liked hot peppers.

> Beware of false prophets, who come to you in sheep's clothing, but inwardly are ravenous wolves. You will know them by their fruits. Are grapes gathered from thorns, or figs from thistles? ... Every tree that does not bear good fruit is cut down and thrown into the fire. Thus you will know them by their fruit. (Matthew 7:15–16, 7:19–20)

Our inattention had led us to plant something we didn't want in our garden. It needed to go—immediately and totally. Since this was a matter of taste, we could give it to a friend. If they had been poisonous, we would have thrown them all away.

Sometimes, our inattention allows bad fruit to grow in our lives. Sometimes, it's difficult to tell the false prophets from the real ones. Often the plants can look similar, but the fruit is different.

Jesus commands us to judge not, to be loving and forgiving, to understand that all sin is equal and your sin is no worse than mine, to know that all have sinned and God is willing to forgive all sin. Jesus also calls us to be discerning about who we listen to, who we follow, and what we plant in our spiritual gardens. It's not always clear. Sometimes our inattention leads us astray; sometimes there is deception at work.

So once the bad fruit becomes obvious, dig up that plant, cut down that tree, and get it out of your garden, be that resentment, anger, lust, cynicism, or divisiveness.

And sometimes, the issue is not bad fruit, but no fruit at all.

We tried to grow blueberries for three years without success. We researched varieties and growing recommendations. We enhanced the soil and protected the plants, six blueberries in three years. Finally, it was time to dedicate that garden space to something else.

Jesus tells a parable about a similar situation: "For three years I have come looking for fruit on this tree, and still I find none. Cut it down! Why should it waste the soil?" (Luke 13:7). In the parable, the gardener (presumably Jesus) shows grace and convinces the land owner to give the fig tree more time.

What a gift, what a blessing, what a warning.

> The Lord is not slow about his promise, as some think of slowness, but is patient with you, not wanting any to perish, but all to come to repentance. But the day of the Lord will come like a thief. (2 Peter 3:9–10)

Bad fruit is scary. No fruit is disheartening. The fruit of the Spirit is marvelous, enriching, glorious, eternal.

What kind of fruit are you producing?

Wealth

I remember our dining room table covered with tomatoes. Nick said it made him feel wealthy. We were so grateful for God's abundance.

This year, my garden has blessed some squirrels with a wealth of tomatoes.

The heat has been too much for my exuberant cucumbers, and the vines are dying.

I have not given up hope. I still water and tend; there are still blossoms. I have reinforced the fence and netting. If it cools a little and rains a little, I may still get a harvest.

Any harvest fills me with gratitude. What an amazing gift—food from the earth. We are so accustomed to it that the wonder has dulled. God gives us what we need to survive. He always has. Not the government, not business ventures—the earth. God's creation feeds God's creatures.

> God said, "See, I have given you every plant yielding seed that is upon the face of the earth, and every tree with seed in its fruit; you shall have them for food." (Genesis 1:29)

This year, in a time of drought and heat, God has been feeding His wild animals through my garden. That is okay. They cannot go to the grocery store or the farmers' market to purchase what they need. I am grateful that I can.

I am grateful that I have a yard. I am grateful that there are wild animals living among us. I am grateful for water to quench my thirst, trees to provide shade, and a home with air conditioning to keep me cool.

There is so much to be thankful for! So many of God's gifts to us have become *given* that we fail to stop and give thanks for them:

the sun, the warmth, the rain, the cool breeze, water, trees, flowers, grass, seed-bearing fruit.

> You cause the grass to grow for the cattle, and plants for people to use, to bring forth food from the earth. (Psalm 104:14)

Too often I focus on what I want to do and my failure to complete it, and miss what God is accomplishing. I miss the opportunity to give God thanks for what He has provided and for what He is doing in my life.

> Then Jesus asked, "Were not ten made clean? But the other nine, where are they? Was none of them found to return and give praise to God except this foreigner?" (Luke 17:17–18)

Today, I am giving thanks for my peppers. I am choosing not to dwell on my lack of ripe tomatoes. I am grateful for the cucumbers I harvested last month. I have decided to be grateful that my ripening tomatoes may have helped some desperate animal.

> Give thanks in all circumstances, for this is the will of God in Christ Jesus for you. (1 Thessalonians 5:18)

A friend of mine has a sign in her kitchen that reads, "What if you woke up tomorrow with only those things for which you were grateful today?" Would we not spend the entire day listing all the things for which we are grateful? Will I spend at least part of my day today thanking God and being grateful for His gifts? Will you?

Don't you think He would like at least one of us to "return and give praise to God"?

Not So Fast!

Just like Lee Corso on *GameDay*, God is reminding me I don't have the last say about my garden.

It has rained every day, and moments of cool wet weather have revived my plants. My once-wilted tomatoes are showing signs of life. New green tomatoes are growing on the few surviving stalks. I was ready to pull them all up, but wait! Not so fast, Betsy. There is growth here; there is fruit here.

Isn't God amazing!? Just when I thought my garden was dried up and lifeless, there is life! There is fruit!

Perhaps God bringing dead things back to life should not surprise me. He certainly has a history of doing so. Yet it always amazes me! Such joy! Such hope! How can pessimism survive in the face of such evidence?

These new green tomatoes on my dying plant remind me that with God, all things are possible. If He can create the cosmos with a word and man with a breath, of course, He can create new tomatoes on a dying plant. Of course, He can revitalize a lagging congregation. Of course, He can reunite disputing factions. Of course, He can breathe energy into a seemingly hopeless situation. Of course, He can!

> Now to him who by the power at work within us is able to accomplish abundantly far more than all we can ask or imagine, to him be glory in the church and in Christ Jesus to all generations, forever and ever. Amen. (Ephesians 3:20–21)

I am often ready to give up and move on—not just with my garden, but with all kinds of things. How many times have I set a deadline and moved on when others did not meet it? Is this efficiency or impatience? Does this tendency indicate practical realism or cynical unbelief?

My parents, German to the bone, managed our family of eight by enforcing strict schedules. If we were to leave at five, we left at five, whether you were ready or not. I still get anxious if I know I am running late. I try to be more gracious with others, but I still fight the urge to give up and move on when others are not on my schedule.

God is working on this in me. He is not on my schedule. If He has a schedule, He alone sets it. There is a rhythm to life that He has given us based on the rotations of the earth around the sun, but I sense He is not bound by that. Seasons and laws of nature are a gift to us, not a restriction on Him.

So even though it is September, I have little green tomatoes on my aging plants. Even though I am a widow in my sixties, I have started a blog and am learning how to write. Even though you may feel used up, tired, and dying, God can produce something new and wonderful in your life.

> If the Spirit of him who raised Jesus from the dead dwells in you, he who raised Christ from the dead will give life to your mortal bodies also through his Spirit who dwells in you. (Romans 8:11)

And this life is not merely eternal; it is full and vibrant in the here and now. Life with Christ is like new tomatoes on an old plant. His Spirit within gives me the ability to be patient and flexible in my dealings with others, and with myself. He makes me hopeful and expectant rather than cynical and pessimistic.

I am glad I had not pulled the plants already, given up on them, and moved on. God still had life for them to live. God still has life for me to live. God still has life for you to live.

> I came that they may have life, and have it abundantly. (John 10:10)

Trapped

I went to pull down the bird netting this morning and found a bird trapped inside the netting. Frantic at my presence, she flew to the netting to try to get out.

Since I was taking down the netting anyway, I just went about getting it down. Surely, she would notice the open sides as I pulled the netting away.

But she didn't. As I opened foot after foot of freedom, she flew a few feet in front of me, madly beating at the netting. As I rounded the garden space, she clung to the netting until she was at the end, trapped in the mesh. The entire garden was open. If she had not clung to the netting, she could have been free much earlier.

The bird netting is collected and balled together at the ends. When she reached the end, she became entangled, unable to free herself. Calmly and softly, and against her loud protests, I cut the mesh away from her. Finally, the netting was away from her wings, and she flew free.

> Christ has set us free. Stand firm, therefore, and do not submit again to a yoke of slavery. (Galatians 5:1)

Do we do the same? Trapped inside a net of bad behaviors, do we cling to what we know, frantic to escape but unable to see the freedom available to us? Do we seek to escape through the very means by which we were trapped?

What entanglements am I clinging to instead of trusting in Jesus? Am I looking to Him or trying to save myself? Do I, like the bird, miss the available path to freedom?

The entire garden was open, but this poor bird was trapped in the netting bunched in one spot. My presence with the scissors drew vehement protests, but eventually, I cut away the entanglements and set her free.

Has not God done the same for me? Such a life of freedom and joy awaits if I can just look away from the netting and fly free. When sin has ensnared me, have I complained as God cut away the trap? What great lengths God has gone to free me!

> For God so loved the world that he gave his only Son, so that everyone who believes in him may not perish but may have eternal life. (John 3:16)

What joy I felt when the bird finally flew away. The netting was there to protect the tomatoes; I didn't want a bird entangled and injured by it. My heart ached as she struggled in vain to free herself. If my selfish heart can care so much for this bird's plight, how much more must God's heart ache for us? How He must rejoice when we finally let Him save us!

> Just so, I tell you, there will be more joy in heaven over one sinner who repents than over ninety-nine righteous persons who need no repentance. (Luke 15:7)

Once the bird flew free, she had her friends and the entire neighborhood at her disposal. Unencumbered by the netting, her options seemed limitless.

What is trapping you today? What is trapping me? God wants to set us free. He does not want to see us die in our sins. He has created a beautiful world for us with seemingly limitless options. Will you let Him set you free?

> So if the Son makes you free, you will be free indeed. (John 8:36)

Sharing

The bird netting is down. For me, that declares the end of my tomato season. There are still green tomatoes on the vine, but I am sharing them with the wildlife that calls my backyard home. My last harvested tomato is ripening on my table. Soon it will be a delicious sandwich, my last until next summer.

I struggle a little with not picking every possible tomato from my garden. It feels wasteful. There is a part of me that feels I should gather as much as I can and leave nothing to waste. Could this be greed and a result of scarcity fears? And is it really a waste to let the animals have some tomatoes? Didn't God grow plants for them as well?

When God through Moses established a covenant community agreement with his people, He made sharing the last of the crop a law.

> When you reap the harvest of your land, you shall not reap to the very edges of your field, or gather the gleanings of your harvest. You shall not strip your vineyard bare, or gather the fallen grapes of your vineyard; you shall leave them for the poor and the alien: I am the Lord your God. (Leviticus 19:9–10)

I don't have any poor or alien people in my backyard, nor do I have a big enough garden to invite them in. But I do have wildlife: birds, bunnies, foxes, coyotes, squirrels, and chipmunks. I can share God's gifts with them.

Can I expand this act of sharing to other areas of my life? Can I live with my hands more open?

Jesus lived that way. He was not concerned over matching linens or marble countertops. He was not concerned about gathering up as much as He could while He could.

When the disciples gave him five loaves, He shared it with five thousand people (Matthew 14, Mark 6, Luke 9, and John 6) He shared His time and His life generously with all people. He instructed us to give to everyone who asks (Matthew 5), not to worry about food and clothing (Matthew 6), and to lay up our treasures in heaven not on earth (Mathew 6).

Amazing things can happen when we follow God's directives to share what He has given us.

Boaz was a landowner simply following God's gleaning laws, when he noticed Ruth, probably the most famous gleaner in the Bible.

> She is the Moabite who came back with Naomi from the country of Moab. She said, "Please let me glean and gather behind the reapers." So she has come, and she has been on her feet from early this morning until now, without resting for even a moment. (Ruth 2:6–7)

Ruth, the foreign woman working in the field, great-grandmother to King David.

Gleaning takes many forms in today's economy. Some nonprofit organizations still glean the fields of commercial farms to add to food banks. Many grocery stores and restaurants donate unused foodstuffs to homeless shelters. Some businesses intentionally hire disabled workers and ex-convicts, giving them dignity and a living wage. Many companies donate goods, services, and profits to help others.

Do I really need *everything* my field produces? Could there be someone who needs at least a little of it more than I do?

> Whoever has two coats must share with anyone who has none; and whoever has food must do likewise. (Luke 3:11)

Open your hand today. Share what God has given you. And watch our amazing God at work.

Tithing

Tithing, like gleaning, was a harvest law established when the people of God entered the Promised Land.

> Set apart a tithe of all the yield of your seed that is brought in yearly from the field. (Deuteronomy 14:22)

The people were to eat this annual tithe in a communal feast, in the presence of the Lord, at the place that God chose "so that you may learn to fear the Lord your God always" (Deuteronomy 14:23).

> Every third year you shall bring out the full tithe of your produce for that year, and store it within your towns; the Levites, because they have no allotment or inheritance with you, as well as the resident aliens, the orphans and the widows in your towns, may come and eat their fill so that the Lord your God may bless you in all the work that you undertake. (Deuteronomy 14:28–29)

This is the tithe that most churchgoers know. Ten percent of our earnings go to the church for support of the staff and facility and for charitable gifts to the community and the world.

The Levites, like the foreigners, widows, and orphans, did not have land allotted to them by Joshua. Therefore, they had no means of providing food for themselves. The Levites instead were to dedicate themselves to the service of God, the care of the temple, and the offering of sacrifices.

> To the Levites, I have given every tithe in Israel for a possession in return for the service that

they perform, the service in the tent of meeting. (Numbers 18:21)

How the Levites handled this influx of grain and wine, who got how much and why, is not known, but Moses instructs them to "set apart an offering from it to the Lord, a tithe of the tithe" (Numbers 18:26).

God, through Moses, set up tithing as an obligation, not as a charitable act, more like the taxes that support our first responders, teachers, and civil servants. Unlike countries with state religions, our taxes do not support our religious institutions, but God still calls us, as the people of God, to support them.

> Bring the full tithe into the storehouse, so that there may be food in my house, and thus put me to the test, says the Lord of hosts; see if I will not open the windows of heaven for you and pour down for you an overflowing blessing. (Malachi 3:10)

We live in a time of financial disclosure, salary negotiations, and 501(c)3s. We review how nonprofits and businesses use the money they receive; we demand tax returns from our candidates for office. Do we monitor how we spend our own resources as closely as we monitor how others spend theirs?

Are we bringing the full tithe into the warehouse? Are we supporting those who are maintaining our temples and offering their service to God? Are we presenting our tithe to the Lord, at the place of His choosing, so that we remember to fear the Lord?

> Take care that you do not forget the Lord your God. When you have eaten your fill and have built fine houses and live in them, ... and all you have is multiplied, then do not exalt yourself, forgetting the Lord your God ... Do not say to yourself, "My power and the might of own hand has gotten me this

wealth." But remember the Lord your God, for it is he who gives you power to get wealth. (Deuteronomy 8:12, 8:14, 8:17–18)

For where your treasure is, there your heart will be also. (Matthew 6:21)

October

My garden is rather feral now. I am not watering it or weeding it or tending to it. Nor have I pulled up my plants and prepared for winter. My garden is in recess, a time of unstructured play. My pepper plants seem quite happy about this. Innately able to withstand hotter, drier temperatures, they seem to revel in the occasional rain and cooler nights.

I planted my peppers at the same time I planted my cucumbers and tomatoes. The cucumber plants have been dead for many weeks. One lone tomato plant is hanging on, still producing, but all the rest are just brown stalks.

But these peppers, these proud elderly denizens of my garden still declare that God is not done yet!

> Now to him who by the power at work within us is able to accomplish abundantly far more than all we can ask or imagine, to him be the glory in the church and in Jesus Christ to all generations, forever and ever. Amen. (Ephesians 3:20–21)

I confess that I find it difficult to move this concept from my head to my heart. Abundantly more than I can imagine? My head says God is capable of anything and everything. My heart cautions me to keep my expectations low to minimize my disappointment.

Faith tells me that whatever God does in my life He does with the purpose of bringing me to a closer relationship with Him, whether it aligns with my expectations and desires or not.

And being able to have a close personal relationship with the creator of the universe is a truly amazing thing! He spoke our planet and all life on it into existence; He spoke through His prophets,

His angels, and His Son; and He speaks through His Spirit today. He called life into existence, and He calls me by name. Why be disappointed if my puny plans don't work out the way I had imagined? He is able to accomplish far more, abundantly far more.

Watching these peppers ripen in mid-October boosts my faith and makes me yearn for longer-living plants, bushes, or trees even. Wouldn't it be nice if my plants didn't die and could regrow on their own next year? I love the fruit these annual plants bear, but I long for hardier, more deeply rooted vegetation. I see the allure of apple groves and pecan stands, blueberry bushes and fig plants.

To grow those plants takes a bigger commitment than my summer garden requires: more space, more time, more patience. Sometimes I find it difficult to wait two months for fruit; could I wait five years? If I am that impatient with my garden, am I that impatient with God?

> The Lord is not slow about his promise, as some think of slowness, but is patient with you, not wanting any to perish but all to come to repentance. (2 Peter 3:9)

If I were to plant a pear tree today, there is a chance that I would not be able to pick its fruit when it came in five years. Then again, the only way I can have pears in five years is to plant the tree today. Perhaps the fruit would be for someone else to harvest.

I hope that I am not a shallow plant, short-lived and easily uprooted. I hope that I have put down deep roots, found hidden streams of water, and bear eternal fruit. But my garden is full of short-lived shallow plants, which bear wonderful fruit, feeding me, my friends, and the animals. Perhaps God's garden needs all of them, all of us.

Perhaps if I am rooted in God, He will provide fruit long after I expect Him to, even into late October, even after I am able to harvest it.

Pesto

My basil leaves are turning yellow. The bright green leaves are duller today; perhaps the shorter days are causing this. Even their scent seems muted. I love the flavor of basil, so I am going to harvest these leaves today while they are still green. I will make pesto.

Gardening has taught me that procrastination is rarely a good plan. Every day, something is different than it was yesterday. The cucumber you let grow another day yellows and sours. The broccoli you leave for tomorrow blossoms overnight. The basil left for a few more days browns and withers. You must watch these plants closely and act when the time is right.

> See, now is the acceptable time; see, now is the day of salvation. (2 Corinthians 6:2)

What fruit is God bringing forth in my life that I need to use *today*? What act of care, what expression of comfort, what word of support needs to happen *today*?

There may be obstacles in the way. There were in my pesto making. My food processor died, full of half-made pesto. Additional leaves had been cut; I needed to make the pesto that day. My first couple of phone calls went unanswered. Then I remembered my sister who was only in town for a few days, staying at her son's home.

Instead of losing my pesto and my patience struggling with unwieldy appliances, I went to her son's house. We made five batches of pesto and shared an enjoyable time working together. There was more than just pesto made that morning!

> Two are better than one, because they have a good reward for their toil. For if they fall, one will lift up the other; but woe to one who is alone and falls and does not have another to help. (Ecclesiastes 4:9–10)

I love that the organizers of the Bible titled this section "The Value of a Friend." As a widow living alone, I could let fear and failure and falling dictate my life. But I don't. I have friends, and family that are friends, and I am not alone. Even when my problems are comparatively minor in scope, like a failing food processor, when I work with another, I can have a good reward for my toil.

And the comfort of friendly support and a shared experience is even more treasured than the pesto!

Sometimes the process of working together is more important than the project. As a task-oriented individual, I feel I should tell myself this every day. My relationships are more important than my to-do list. Your needs may well be of greater importance than my plans. God has put me in this time and place for a reason (Esther 4:15). Perhaps that reason is to be with you right now.

> Do nothing from selfish ambition or conceit, but in humility regard others as better than yourselves. Let each of you look not to your own interests, but to the interest of others. (Philippians 2:3–4)

I am grateful that my sister was available to help me make pesto before the leaves wilted. I am grateful that someone invented pesto to preserve that wonderful basil taste long after the plants rested. I am grateful that I will get to reap the benefits of my basil in the future, because I acted, with help, at the right time.

Even as much as I will enjoy this pesto in the future, I think the story of how my sister rescued me that morning will last longer. Isn't that the way with God? What we accomplish may last a while; what He accomplishes lasts much longer, maybe forever.

End-Times

Some of my Christian friends think we are in the end-times. My garden is in the end-times. The tomato plants have turned brown and wilted. The cucumber leaves are yellowed and curled. No new fruit is evident. Only the weeds seem to thrive.

Yes, this is the end-times for my garden. And yet it is not. Next year, God willing, I will have another garden. It won't be exactly like this one. Every year, my garden is a little different. Every year, some plants flourish and others struggle.

What looks like the end is just change. Change can be scary, but it is certainly nothing new. Change may indicate the end of some beloved patterns, but it has yet to indicate The End.

> And you will hear of wars and rumors of wars; see that you are not alarmed; for this must take place, but the end is not yet. (Matthew 24:6)

Since Jesus spoke those words, Rome has fallen, the Holy Roman Empire has fallen, the Ottoman Empire has fallen, and The Soviet Union has fallen. Will the US fall? History teaches us it is bound to happen at some point.

But as Christians, we have a dual citizenship. Even if our nation changes radically, even if our nation falls, our status as citizens of God's kingdom will not change. His empire will never fall.

> But our citizenship is in heaven, and it is from there that we are expecting a Savior, the Lord Jesus Christ. (Philippians 3:20)

Yes, our world is changing; so is my garden. My garden is dying; soon it will be dead, for a season. Since I have a longer concept of time than my plants, I know that this is just a time of rest. The garden will be back next year. It will be different, sure, maybe better, maybe not, but this is not the end of all gardening.

Imagine how much larger God's concept of time is than ours. Eternity. What is four hundred years? What is a thousand? What is four thousand? God called Abram roughly four thousand years ago.

> But do not ignore this one fact, beloved, that with the Lord one day is like a thousand years, and a thousand years are like one day. (2 Peter 3:8)

Yes, my garden is ending. This change is not a cause for fear or distress. Perhaps it is an opportunity to examine myself and see where I have put my confidence.

Am I trusting my efforts in my garden to feed me? Don't I know that God alone can make a tomato grow? Am I trusting in our government to eradicate evil in our society? Don't I know that God alone can overcome evil? Don't I know that Jesus Christ alone is my Savior?

> Some take pride in chariots, and some in horses, but our pride is in the name of the Lord our God. They will collapse and fall, but we shall rise and stand upright. (Psalm 20:7–8)

If this is the end-times, let us take the opportunity today to put our confidence in God and take pride only in His saving grace. If this is just a change of seasons, putting our confidence in God alone will prepare us to embrace God's gifts in the new season.

May the peace of Christ be with you.

Food

It's November. If you live in the United States, that means Thanksgiving is near. If you do not live in the United States, you are missing a wonderful celebration of God's abundant provisions. Thanksgiving is the only holiday that is celebrated in no other way but by the gathering of family and friends to eat and eat abundantly. It is a celebration of our thankfulness for food.

From the beginning, God knew we needed food and provided it, perhaps even creating this need in us.

> God said, "See, I have given you every plant yielding seed that is upon the face of all the earth, and every tree with seed in its fruit; you shall have them for food." (Genesis 1:29)

When His people were wandering around the wilderness, God provided manna for them to eat and occasionally quail.

Food was a necessary part of hospitality, and feasting was a national requirement for the Israelites. There were many reasons to sacrifice animals to the Lord; most involved a subsequent feast.

> And the flesh of your thanksgiving sacrifice of well-being shall be eaten on the day it is offered; you shall not leave any of it until morning. (Leviticus 7:15)

Food played a critical role in Jesus's ministry—from meals with sinners and Pharisees, to the feeding of thousands. Jesus compared the kingdom of heaven to a feast (Matthew 22, Luke 14) and used yeast to describe both bad teaching (Mark 8) and the kingdom of God (Luke 13).

Jesus establishes the most enduring remembrance of His life, death, and return as a meal: the Last Supper, the Lord's Supper, Holy Communion, Eucharist.

> Then he took a loaf of bread, and when he had given thanks, he broke it and gave it to them, saying, "This is my body, which is given for you. Do this in remembrance of me." (Luke 22:19)

Food. We must have it. We have made an art form of it. Just the varieties of bread across cultures and within cultures are mind-boggling. A friend of mine makes egg rolls for Thanksgiving to honor her Vietnamese heritage. Naan is a wonderful addition to crescent rolls. How about leftover turkey tacos or pitas along with our hot browns? How many varieties of dressing does your family serve?

> Jesus said to them, "I am the bread of life. Whoever comes to me will never be hungry, and whoever believes in me will never be thirsty." (John 6:35)

As wonderful and filling as our Thanksgiving feast may be, by the next day, we will need more food. But once we know Jesus, crucified and risen, we do not need to know anything else. We have abundance.

> I came that they may have life, and have it abundantly. (John 10:10)

We have much to be thankful for, many gifts, much grace.

Preparing a Feast

Many of us, in mid-November, are preparing a feast.

Soon, family and friends will gather for what is traditionally the biggest feast day on the American calendar. No hamburgers and hotdogs here!

Preparing for Thanksgiving takes planning and coordination. Who is coming? Where will they sit? What are their dietary restrictions? What side dish can they bring to the table?

What can I buy in advance? What can I cook in advance? What must be cooked on Thursday? What is the schedule for the oven? What dishes do I use to serve the food? What plates and silverware will I use?

Centerpiece? Tablecloth? Napkins? Place cards?

God is preparing a feast for us.

> I tell you, many will come from east and west and will eat with Abraham and Isaac and Jacob in the kingdom of heaven. (Matthew 8:11)

He has been preparing this feast for us, the human race, for a long time, and it promises to be glorious.

And unlike my dining room table, there is plenty of room.

The problem seems to be that some people have made other plans. We've had the years when Thanksgiving looked like that. My sister was visiting her husband's family; my daughter was traveling with her in-laws; my son was working on Wednesday and Friday and couldn't make the trip. Suddenly, my table looked empty.

> Then Jesus said to him, "Someone gave a great dinner and invited many. At the time for the dinner he sent his slave to those who had been invited, 'Come; for

> everything is ready now.' But they all alike began to make excuses." (Luke 14:16–18)

One of those years when no one was able to come, I went to Atlanta to spend Thanksgiving with my family there. Our God, through Jesus, does this too. He comes to us when we are making excuses for why we can't go to Him.

> Listen! I am standing at the door, knocking; if you hear my voice and open the door, I will come into you and eat with you, and you with me. (Revelation 3:20)

He wants to have this great feast with us.
He modeled it in Mosaic law.

> Speak to the people of Israel saying: On the fifteenth day of this seventh month, and lasting seven days, there shall be the feast of booths to the Lord." (Leviticus 23:34)

Not just a feast on one day, but a feast for seven days, a *huge* feast—for everyone.

God gave David a vision of a feast with his enemies present, where they would have to acknowledge God's blessing of his life (Psalm 23:5).

And Jesus loved to feast—with sinners, which is a good thing because it means we, the sinners, are welcome.

> When the scribes of the Pharisees saw that he was eating with sinners and tax collectors, they said to his disciples, "Why does he eat with tax collectors and sinners?" When Jesus heard this, he said to them, "Those who are well have no need of a physician, but those who are sick; I have come to call not the righteous but sinners." (Mark 2:16–17)

So as I am preparing my feast for my family, I remember that God is preparing a feast for humankind and inviting all the sinners to celebrate with him. What a glorious feast that will be!

> And the angel said to me, "Write this: Blessed are those who are invited to the marriage supper of the Lamb." And he said to me, "These are true words of God." (Revelation 19:9)

Enjoy the feast!

Giving Thanks

Today, let me lift my voice in thanks to God.

Thank You, Lord, that I can write these words and send them out.

Thank You, Lord, that someone is reading these words.

Thank You for computers and electricity and the written word and teachers who taught us to read and write.

Thank You for the printing press and those dedicated souls who copied Your word by hand.

Thank You, Lord, for giving us Your word in written form.

> All scripture is inspired by God and is useful for teaching, for reproof, for correction, and for training in righteousness. (2 Timothy 3:16)

Thank You, Lord, for ample food easily available.

Thank You for the people who grew this food, raised these animals, ensured their quality, transported them, and kept them unspoiled for us.

Thank You for the generations before us who taught us how to prepare this food and gave us recipes to follow.

Thank You for the variety of tastes and flavors and combinations that your natural world provides for us.

Thank You for the different cultures who have influenced what we cook, how we cook, and how we eat our food.

> Then people will come from east and west, from north and south, and will eat in the kingdom of God. (Luke 13:29)

Thank You, Lord, that I am healthy enough to prepare this food and my family is healthy enough to join me.

Thank You for medicines that cure, medicines that treat, and medicines that prevent.

Thank You for the scientists and doctors who develop those medicines.

Thank You that medicines can be delivered to my door or picked up in minutes.

Thank You for doctors who have taken the time and energy to understand the human body and diseases and disorders.

Thank You for their teachers who have shared the knowledge gained from previous generations who cared for the sick.

> "And when was it that we saw you sick or in prison and visited you?" And the king will answer them, "Truly I tell you, just as you did it to one of the least of these who are members of my family, you did it to me." (Matthew 25:39–40)

Thank You, Lord, that my family is able to join me in giving thanks to You.

Thank You for family.

Thank You for uniting these people born to different sets of parents into one family that could gather together to thank You.

Thank You for parents who love their children.

Thank You for children who care for their parents.

Thank You for the circumstances in life that brought us all to this table.

> Give thanks in all circumstances; for this is the will of God in Christ Jesus for you. (1 Thessalonians 5:18)

Thank You, Lord, for your earth around us.

Thank You for frosty nights and warm houses.

Thank You for leaves that turn red and brown and, in the spring, green again.

Thank You for sunlit clouds and the radiant colors of sunrises and sunsets.

Thank You for flowers that bloom in the winter, bringing color to our world.

> And one called to another and said, "Holy, holy, holy is the Lord of hosts; the whole earth is full of his glory." (Isaiah 6:3)

Thank You, Lord, for this day set aside to give thanks.

Thank You for reminding us that we did not create this world; You did.

Thank You for reminding us that the sun, the rain, the ground, the plants, the animals, our bodies, our brains, and whatever abilities we have, all are a gift from You.

Thank You for sending your Son to draw us closer to You.

Thank You for caring so much for us, for loving us even when we are unlovable.

Thank You for forgiving us even though it cost so much.

Thank You for the opportunity to call You Lord and Father.

> Praise the Lord, all you nations! Extol him, all you peoples! For great is his steadfast love toward us, and the faithfulness of the Lord endures forever. Praise the Lord! (Psalm 117)

Winter Rest

Winter is a time of rest when God calls His creation to cease from their labors. Winter is when God replenishes the earth.

My beloved had a vineyard on a very fertile hill. He dug it and cleared it of stones, and planted it with choice vines; he built a watchtower in the midst of it, and hewed out a wine vat in it. He expected it to yield grapes, but it yielded wild grapes. And now, inhabitants of Jerusalem and people of Judah, judge between me and my vineyard. What more was there to do for my vineyard that I have not done in it? When I expected it to yield grapes, why did it yield wild grapes? For the vineyard of the Lord of hosts is the house of Israel, and the people of Judah are his pleasant planting; he expected justice, but saw bloodshed; righteousness, but heard a cry! (Isaiah 5:1–4, 5:7)

"Listen to another parable. There was a landowner who planted a vineyard, put a fence around it, dug a wine press in it, and built a watchtower. Then he leased it to tenants and went to another country. When the harvest time had come, he sent his slaves to the tenants to collect his produce. But the tenants seized his slaves and beat one, killed another, and stoned another. Again he sent other slaves, more than the first; and they treated them in the same way. Finally he sent his son to them, saying, 'They will respect my son.' But when the tenants saw the son, they said to themselves, 'This is the heir; come, let us kill him and get his inheritance.' So, they seized him, threw him out of the vineyard, and killed him. Now when the owner of the vineyard comes, what will he do to those tenants?" (Matthew 21:33–40, also Mark 12:1–9, Luke 20:9–15)

Garlic Scapes

The planting instructions warned that the garlic bulbs might send up sprouts in the spring. Imagine my surprise to see them now! Someone who lived farther north must have written the instructions; in Tennessee, we have warm sunny spells throughout the winter.

Fortunately, I had wandered out to the garden in the days after Thanksgiving, something I do every few weeks during the winter. And look! Garlic scapes!

The instructions are quite clear: cut them off. Until next summer, all the nutrients need to stay in the bulb, not transfer above ground.

So I cut all the scapes off the garlic bulbs.

I felt a little cruel, snipping off these efforts to reach for the sun, rudely ending the plants' attempts to grow.

But it is not their time. As a gardener trying to grow garlic bulbs, it is my responsibility to nip this instinctive urge to grow in the bud. They are doing what they are meant to do, and doing it well. But the timing is not right.

I know that there are winter months ahead. I know that the bulbs need to store their nutrients. I know that these bulbs need more time in the quiet earth before they can reach their full potential.

I wonder if the bulbs consider me a cruel and vengeful gardener who is denying them success or if they can trust that I have a better plan for them.

Can I trust that God has a better plan for me?

> For my thoughts are not your thoughts, nor are your ways my ways, says the Lord. For as the heavens are higher than the earth, so are my ways higher than your ways, and my thoughts than your thoughts. (Isaiah 55:8–9)

The Advent season is all about waiting until God says the time is right.

The Jewish people had to wait five hundred years for God to fulfill His vision given to Isaiah of the Messiah's birth. We are still waiting for the peaceable kingdom and the new heaven and new earth.

It makes me think of the wrapped presents under the tree. They are there. They are for us. One day, the gift inside will be ours. But not today—it's not the right time yet.

Sometimes, I have gotten all excited about something and shared it with the world, who had little or no interest in it. I'd like to think I was sending up garlic scapes: good things, wrong time.

> Humble yourselves therefore under the mighty hand of God, so that he may exalt you in due time. (1 Peter 5:6)

It is my job to help it do so by cutting off its desire to show itself before its time.

And God has rewarded me for making the garlic wait for the right time. I have delicious garlic scapes to add to my leftover turkey and dressing, and more to add to every dish I cook. They are a wonderful addition to eggs, pasta, burgers, and potatoes.

What probably looks like dashed hopes and failure to the garlic bulb, God is using to bless my life today and ensure a larger role for the garlic bulb in the future.

Ready and Waiting

I have finished preparing my home for Christmas. Everything is ready for what's next. Now I must wait.

It's tempting to add more things to the list, to keep the adrenaline pumping. Nature abhors a vacuum, and the Protestant work ethic abhors an empty list. And of course, there is always more I *could* do, but I am choosing not to.

Today, I will get a cup of hot chocolate, listen to Amy Grant's music, maybe even get a fire going in the fireplace.

Is this just age, the aftereffects of an autumn of illness throughout my family, a month of surgeries and falls and heartbreaks among my friends? It's almost as if God has been reminding me how to be still, be quiet, be at home, lessons I learned during COVID-19 then promptly forgot.

And while waiting is difficult, I find it somehow comforting to be *ready* and waiting. I am not anxious. I can see God's hand in preparing me for all that has come before; I can sense God's hand preparing me for what is to come.

More and more, I am convinced that my only real task is to share God's love with those around me, and everything else is secondary. Whether my plans succeed or fail, whether I succeed or fail only matters to the extent that I show love through my actions.

> If I have prophetic powers, and understand all mysteries and all knowledge, and if I have all faith, so as to remove mountains, but do not have love, I am nothing. (1 Corinthians 13:2)

If I am busy showing love as best I can to those around me, then I can be confident that when the master returns, whenever that may be, he will find me at my task (Mark 13:32–37). Not that I have it all figured out or am always the easiest person to be around, but God has told us what He wants from us, and there is peace in that.

> He has told you, O mortal, what is good; and what does the Lord require of you but to do justice, and to love kindness, and to walk humbly with your God? (Micah 6:8)

Because we mortals are so very bad at following even these simple directions, Jesus came to live among us as a fellow mortal, to show us how to do it, even better than a YouTube video. And He stands for us in heaven, forgiving our failures, sending His Spirit to guide and strengthen us, allowing us entry. What a friend we have in Jesus!

So instead of rushing around completing a million little tasks that might impress my friends and family, I am choosing to wait on the Lord. Read His Word. Love His children. Commune with His Spirit. Listen for His guidance.

And in the stillness, in the quiet, I not only sense peace, I also sense joy and love, His presence.

For He has come; He comes still; He will come again. May He find us all ready and waiting when He does.

Happy Advent and Merry Christmas!

Be Patient

> Be patient, therefore, beloved, until the coming of the Lord. The farmer waits for the precious crop from the earth, being patient with it until it receives the early and the late rains. You also must be patient. (James 5:7–8)

This verse has been rumbling around in my brain throughout Advent. I am not sure what exactly I need patience for or about, but I think the Lord wants me to be patient.

Perhaps it is just a reminder during this time of year to not get caught up in action plans.

This is precisely the time of year when I like to look back over the past year and begin planning for the new one.

What went well, what didn't? What did God teach me? What did I have to learn the hard way? When did I insist on my own way? How did that work out? Where can I see God at work over the past year?

A year in review, if you will, without the sordid headlines.

A year in review begs the question "What am I going to do differently this year?" If I want to grow something new in my garden, I need to find the space and the time to grow it. If I want to nourish a new area of growth in my life, I need to commit resources to it. But then I hear that verse again.

> The farmer waits for the precious crop from the earth, being patient with it until it receives the early and the late rains. You also must be patient. (James 5:7–8)

Shouldn't I be doing something while I am waiting patiently? In a garden, there is always work to be done. Maybe God is teaching me that I need not worry about the outcome. I do the work; He grows the tomato. The outcome is in His hands.

If my garlic fails because I have now cut garlic scapes three times while it is still winter, then they fail, and I have had delicious garlic scapes to use all winter.

If you all stop reading this because, honestly, how many times do you want to read about the wonder of a seed and the beauty of fruit, then so be it.

If my idea of how long it should take to write a book is years different from how long it actually takes, then I will be patient.

If I have to make a New Year's resolution, something I avoid, it is to continue to plant seeds in faith that God will bring forth fruit when the time is right; to be content if I should sow and another reap; to not worry about the seed that falls on rocky or weedy ground.

Because who knows what tomorrow will bring? Only God.

So, Lord, let me plant good seeds in the New Year. Bring them to fruition in Your time. Help me be patient and wait for the early and late rains. Thank You for the opportunities You give me. Thank You for seeds to plant.

Planning

Planning feels so empowering! Planning is much easier than doing, and I feel like I have accomplished something.

I am not alone in this love of planning. There are entire industries devoted to helping us plan. It's hard to imagine what life was like before there were calendars. The COVID-19 shutdown may have wiped them clean for a while, but I was eager to get back to planning things.

What I have learned, over time and through much frustration, is that I must make plans in pencil, preferably a pencil with a large eraser. This was certainly true while Nick was suffering through surgeries, chemo, and failing health. It has also been true this past fall. Awaiting the birth of twins, their arrival on Thanksgiving week, extended family coming and going with their own plans, some surgeries and biopsies thrown in the mix, why bother owning a pen?

> Come now, you who say, "Today or tomorrow we will go to such-and-such a town and spend a year there, doing business and making money." Yet you do not even know what tomorrow will bring. What is your life? For you are a mist that appears for a little while and then vanishes. (James 4:13–14)

It's a new year. Did you make a New Year's resolution? I admit I stopped making them a long time ago. I eased into it by dubbing the upcoming year "the year of the house" or "the year for travel." But I found that I rarely knew in January what the upcoming year would hold.

Now I make my plans in pencil. I hope to have a garden. I have been scheming on ways to enrich the soil, hinder weeds among the sugar snaps, frustrate the robber squirrels and chipmunks. I plan to continue writing. Maybe I'll have a better garden; hopefully, I'll become a better writer. God willing, I will have some new things to share. I'd like to spend some time at the beach and a lot of time at the lake. I plan to spend time with my grandchildren and my children and my family and my friends, if the Lord wishes.

> Instead, you ought to say, "If the Lord wishes, we will live and do this or that." (James 4:15)

Who besides God knows what the new year will bring—for the world, for our country, for my family, for me? As civil rights activist Ralph Abernathy famously said, "I do not know what the future holds, but I know who holds the future."

That's why I do not stress about not being able to plan in pen. It's a little scary to be open to whatever the Lord may send my way. I make my plans, but I prepare myself for God changing them. I try to leave words like *never* and *always* out of my vocabulary, a hard lesson for people like me. I remind myself that my plans need to be subject to His plans. His plans are better than mine: better for the world, better for His kingdom, better for me.

And He is with us—no matter what happens, to the end of the age.

> Now to him who by the power at work within us is able to accomplish abundantly far more than all we can ask or imagine, to him be glory in the church and in Christ Jesus to all generations, forever and ever. Amen. (Ephesians 3:20–21)

Happy New Year!

Winter in the Garden

A peaceful quiet has descended on my home. The crowds and chaos and cooking and cleaning that mark the holidays are over. The decorations still adorn my home, but they are waiting to return to the attic.

Even my garden is quiet and at rest. Despite the onions growing in my yard and the scapes escaping from my garlic, the cardboard is keeping my garden at rest, like blackout blinds.

Sleep is necessary, rest is necessary, downtime is necessary. Even when the world gives me excessive stimulation. Even when the temperatures reach the sixties in the winter. Even when I sense I should be doing something in the quiet times.

I am doing something, just like my garden is doing something. I am resting. I am processing what has come before and thinking about what is to come. I am slowing my heart rate and lowering my blood pressure. I am resting my muscles and allowing myself to heal.

> He said to them, "Come away to a deserted place all by yourselves and rest a while." For many were coming and going, and they had no leisure even to eat. (Mark 6:31)

Winter is a time when the garden replenishes itself. Potassium and phosphorus from deep in the ground rise to replace the nutrients used by the summer plants. Beneficial microorganisms have time to develop away from the demands of growing plants. The fallow ground regains its nutritional balance after a summer of feeding growth. Winter rest is like Gatorade for the garden, restoring its essential minerals.

Winter rest for the garden is the model for Sabbath rest for us.

> Six days shall work be done, but on the seventh day you shall have a holy sabbath of solemn rest to the Lord. (Exodus 35:2)

The garden needs to rest before I can ask more of it in the spring and summer. I need to rest before God asks more of me. This time of rest increases the likelihood that the garden, and I, will be able to bear fruit in season.

January is my time of rest when my spirit is replenished. Little whispers from God rise to the surface and invigorate me. His presence restores me.

I may need to force this rest upon myself. I may need to put down cardboard to suppress outside distractions. I may need to close the blackout blinds. We are not Energizer bunnies; we need to turn ourselves off. Often we are like the screaming toddler who refuses nap time when nap time is exactly what we need.

It's a new year. Our calendars still have space on them. There is much that could happen, may happen, will happen. There are surprises, good and bad, ahead. I encourage you, as I encourage myself, to take this time to rest. God has got this. Put yourself in His hands, read His Word, listen to His voice, follow His guidance. God will put you where He wants you; God will put me where He wants me. For now, let me rest so I am ready.

> Return, O my soul, to your rest, for the Lord has dealt bountifully with you. (Psalm 116:7)

The Heron

The recent rain had filled my creek with water, awakening the dormant fish eggs hiding beneath the rocks. Enticed by the new life, the heron came to visit. Oblivious to me, the majestic bird concentrated on the water in the creek, looking for a snack-sized fish. I hope she found one. I did not have the patience she showed as she stood for long minutes, watching and waiting. At the beach when I have fewer tasks at hand, I have seen them stand for hours on the beach, waiting for the sunning angler to throw a fish back.

I remember when I saw my first heron, back in a hidden cove on the lake. I thought something had escaped from Jurassic Park. When I see them in numbers large enough to flock, my heart thanks God for bringing these graceful and impressive birds back from the brink of extinction.

What a gift to see them in my yard! What a gift to see the hawks and eagles who have returned to our area. What a gift to see the bluebirds and blue jays and cardinals and chickadees and robins who have never left. What a gift to hear the little sparrows chattering away and the mockingbird singing medleys of his favorite tunes.

> By the streams the birds of the air have their habitation;
> they sing among the branches. (Psalm 104:12)

I am amazed at the wildlife that surrounds me. This is the twenty-first century. We have computers and cell phones and Wi-Fi and AI. But in my yard, I have birds and bunnies and squirrels and chipmunks. Raccoons and possums and skunks outnumber the people living on my street. Deer and coyote wander through my yard, and foxes have raised their kits here. I know there are mice and moles and voles and a million insects in my yard. I have even seen an armadillo amble across my yard, nose to the ground.

Why do I think this is *my* yard?

Has not God created every one of these creatures as surely as He has created me? Has He not given this earth, this patch of green, for them to live on as surely as He has given it to me? Does He not care for them as He cares for me?

> Look at the birds of the air; they neither sow nor reap nor gather into barns, and yet your heavenly Father feeds them. Are you not of more value than they? (Matthew 6:26)

These animals around me call my yard their home. I have grown so used to them being here that I rarely stop to greet them or acknowledge their presence. Only when something unusual happens do I stop and stand in awe, if I happen to be looking and see it.

When the hawk swooped down on the squirrel, when the young bunny approached my docile old cat, when the duck made a nest in my flower bed, when the mother fox barked at me as I neared her hidden kits, then I stop and give thanks for the vibrant community of animals living in my yard.

Perhaps this yard is more theirs than mine. My efforts run more toward limiting their possession of the space than encouraging it. I sometimes feel as if I am carving out a space for myself in their yard. I know that we as humans need to be good stewards of the land and be kind to all living creatures, but sometimes it feels egotistical to think that these animals in my yard are in any way dependent on me. Sometimes it feels just the opposite. I am amazed at what they teach me. Look at all the different species of birds and mammals and insects that call my yard home! Look how well they share the space, how peacefully they (usually) interact.

I hope you get to go outside today and stand in awe of God's creation—both plant and animal, the beauty, the variety, the differing functions and personalities, the amazing world that lives in a yard—that surrounds us. What an awesome world; what an awesome God!

The Victory Garden

When I think about starting my garden, my hands start to sweat and my throat constricts. There are so many things that can go wrong—bad soil, invading weeds, marauding animals, unpredictable weather, my own inattention. Why do I think I can grow vegetables?

Deep breath. Because I have in the past. I have been victorious over all these obstacles for more than thirty years. I can grow vegetables and fruits. That's why I named my website The Victory Garden.

But *victory* is a deceptive word.

On one hand, victory is success, triumph over difficulties.

> No, in all these things we are more than conquerors through him who loved us. (Romans 8:37)

I love the confidence, the faith, the hope that in the end God wins. God has promised us victory over evil (1 John 4: 4), over Satan (Hebrews 2:14), over sin (1 John 3:8), over our own sinful nature (Colossians 2:13), and over our past (2 Corinthians 5:17).

On the other hand, victory implies that there is war, struggle, hardship. Just look at the verses preceding verse 37:

> Who will separate us from the love of Christ? Will hardship, or distress, or persecution, or famine, or nakedness, or peril, or sword? As it is written, "For your sake we are being killed all day long; we are accounted as sheep to be slaughtered." (Romans 8:35–36)

Victory implies battle, and God has promised us that as well. We will face hatred (Matthew 10:22), persecution (John 15:20), the forces of darkness (Ephesians 6:12), trials (1 Peter 4:12), and refinement by fire (1 Peter 1:7).

Perhaps this is how God's people felt as they entered the Promised Land. People already lived there. This ragtag bunch of nomads would have to fight against established strongholds and peoples, some of whom were giants. Just like with us, God had promised them victory, had promised them land, but there were battles ahead.

God's people are in a battle for possession of our souls, humanity's soul. God has promised us victory, but there is a battle. We need to "put on the full armor of God" (Ephesians 6:11) and listen to God's instructions (Judges 7). Tactics will vary based on the enemy we face, the established sin in our lives, but the battle is real.

And there's an uncomfortable truth hidden in the story of God's people entering the Promised Land.

> Now these were the nations the Lord left to test all those in Israel who had no experience of any war in Canaan. (Judges 3:1)

> Therefore, to keep me from being too elated, a thorn was given me in the flesh, a messenger of Satan to torment me. (2 Corinthians 12:7)

There are Canaanites living in the Promised Land. There are weeds in my garden; there are thorns in my flesh. There is sin in my life; there is evil in our midst.

Don't be discouraged by the Canaanites in the land, the sin that seems to never leave your side, the thorn in your flesh, the failings that keep you humble and dependent on God. Perhaps God is leaving them there for a while to help you deepen your relationship with Him.

> The Lord said to Gideon, "The troops with you are too many for me to give the Midianites into their hand. Israel would only take the credit away from me, saying, 'My own hand has delivered me.'" (Judges 7:2)

Three times I appealed to the Lord about this, that it would leave me, but he said to me, "My grace is sufficient for you, for power is made perfect in weakness." (2 Corinthians 12:9)

Keep fighting, my friend. God will bring victory in His time.

i and You

English is the only language in which the personal pronoun I is always capitalized.

I have journaled morning prayers for years—pages and pages of scrawled-out personal prayers to the Almighty about whatever was on my mind. They are not for public consumption and would probably be indecipherable to most people.

From the beginning, I addressed God with a capital letter, "You." Lord, You know what is on my mind. Thank You for listening. It seemed appropriate, even in my personal journal, to capitalize "You." His Royal Majesty. God.

> Thus says the Lord, your Redeemer, who formed you in the womb: I am the Lord, who made all things, who alone stretched out the heavens, who by myself spread out the earth. (Isaiah 44:24)

Somewhere along the way, I stopped capitalizing "i." Maybe it was after seeing one of those window stickers "HE>i" (He is greater than i.) It seemed prideful somehow to give myself the same honor as i was giving God. Quickly, i became accustomed to the lowercase i. The practice was easy in my journal. My computer is a different story. My writing software does not accept my sudden humility!

The English language capitalizes "i" whenever used as a pronoun. English is *the only* language that capitalizes "i" in the middle of a sentence. This would not seem so egotistical if we capitalized other pronouns, like "they" or "he" or "she." But we don't. Only I get that honor. Even "we" doesn't get that honor, as if adding another person lessens our value somehow. It feels very vain to me.

Many languages do have a formal "you" that is used to show respect or recognize the authority of the person being addressed.

English does not even have that. The English language does not deem you as important as I.

> Do nothing from selfish ambition or conceit, but in humility regard others as better than yourselves. (Philippians 2:3)

So not only is He greater than i, but you are at least as important, if not more so, than i.

I wanted to write my blogs using the lowercase i. I tried it out on a few people, but they found it distracting. My writing software constantly tried to correct me. So i stopped, except for this devotional, because i want you to know that i do not consider myself more important than you. And i do not consider either of us as important as God. He is the one who deserves the honor. He is the only one who deserves the capital letters.

If you keep a journal, i would like to challenge you to try this for a while. The practice is a subtle but constant reminder that He is God and i am not.

Beyond that, what does it say about the English language that we capitalize "i" and not "you"? What does it say about us as a people? Has it formed our thinking?

Don't worry, i will return to proper English grammar, as vain as i find it. The purpose of these devotionals, after all, is not to change our language, but to encourage you to speak with God in whatever language you choose.

> Likewise, the Spirit helps us in our weakness; for we do not know how to pray as we ought, but that very Spirit intercedes with sighs too deep for words. (Romans 8:26)

The Way of Grief

Grief came to visit today. As I was planning my garden, planning my trip, cleaning my house, grief came.

I miss Nick. I miss my best friend, my confidant, my lover. I miss his honesty, his support, his demands on my time. Would he approve of the choices I am making?

Am I pursuing activities to keep this grief at a distance? Like an oozing wound, this grief begs to be re-covered. Plan for a trip, write a book, take some classes, work in the garden. Keep my hands and my mind busy. But like the weeds that work their way to the edges of the garden and burst from the sides of the cardboard, grief is forcing its way into the light.

Is grief, like fear, a sign of lagging faith?

Not faith that Nick is in a better place—I feel quite confident that he is complete now in a way he could never be on earth—but faith that I can move forward emotionally without him, faith that God is directing my steps.

I look back on the past four and a half years and know that God has moved me to an unknown land, parted the seas, taught me new skills, and changed me. Dare I say improved me? There was a time when I thought I had lost my enthusiasm forever, but God has given me new opportunities, new hopes, and new dreams. But with those come doubts and, with the doubts, grief. I miss my old life. I miss Nick. I was comfortable revolving my life around his. I liked our life together: our times at the beach, our times on the lake, our times in the garden.

Whew! I need to shake this off. Clean the wound, reapply the bandage. I wanted to write about ordering a raspberry bush with no knowledge if they would grow here. I wanted to write about the beauty of being able to try again with the fig plant since I killed the one last year. I wanted to write about the importance of research and learning and leaning on the knowledge of others.

> Thus says the Lord: Stand at the crossroads, and look, and ask for the ancient paths, where the good way lies; and walk in it, and find rest for your souls. (Jeremiah 6:16)

Perhaps God in His wisdom is telling me that I can apply this to my grief as well as to my raspberry bush.

I remember the books our congregational care committee sent after Nick's death. I remember the grief counseling our associate pastor led. I remember the tears the group of us shed as we tried to come to terms with our new reality. God has held my hand and moved me from that place to this. But once more, I feel I am standing at a crossroads, looking for the good path. I want to walk in it and find rest for my grieving soul.

There are ancient paths the Lord can show me. Grief is nothing new. Moving on with life after the loss of someone dear is nothing new. Grieving for the loss when it may appear that you have already moved on is nothing new. What is new are the footprints my feet may leave on the path. What is new is who God is transforming me to be.

> So we do not lose heart. Even though our outer nature is wasting away, our inner nature is being renewed day by day. (2 Corinthians 4:16)

Grief came to visit today. It showed me a crossroads. It showed me a cross.

There is an ancient path, a good way. Grief cracked open my heart and showed it to me.

> Jesus said to him, "I am the way and the truth and the life. No one comes to the father except through me." (John 14:6)

Busyness

Somewhere along the line, we made busyness a virtue. If you want to silence a conversation, when someone asks you what you do, say "nothing." Even writing it, I feel I need to follow that with disclaimers, reasons, justifications for what must be idleness, sloth, the devil's workshop.

Do we have one day on our calendar that we intentionally leave blank? Can we block off two hours for prayer and communion with God? Sabbath may have once been that way, but by Jesus's time, it was more rule-riddled than most other days. Sunday worship may have once been that way, but it can also be a time of stress and demands, tightly scheduled between other activities.

> Be still and know that I am God! (Psalm 46:10)

I get the sense that busyness is an idol, a false god. Somehow, I feel as if my life has meaning as long as I am too busy to stop to think about it. When I do stop to think about it, I share Solomon's frustrations that all this activity feels like "chasing after wind" (Ecclesiastes) and a waste of time. It's easy to forget what Solomon's father David taught us:

> Unless the Lord builds the house, those who build it
> labor in vain. (Psalm 127:1)

What would our calendars look like if we prayed for guidance before adding anything to it?

> While staying with them, he ordered them to not
> leave Jerusalem, but to wait there for the promise of
> the Father. Then they returned to Jerusalem ... All

> these were constantly devoting themselves to prayer.
> (Acts 1:4, 1:12, 1:14)

Perhaps this is the key, the balance between pointless activity and idle hands. Perhaps I need to start my day with prayer and waiting for the Spirit's guidance and power. Martin Luther famously said that he had so much to do that he'd have to spend the first three hours in prayer. Perhaps if I spent that much time in prayer, God could accomplish amazing feats through me!

Like the barren ground in my garden right now, perhaps a lack of visible activity allows for a vital unseen activity to occur: rest, time in prayer, time reading and thinking about God's Word, internal transformation. Perhaps that and not ceaseless busyness is the way we can better serve the kingdom. It could even be that the greatest work is that which looks like doing nothing.

> In the morning, while it was still very dark, Jesus got up and went out to a deserted place, and there he prayed. (Mark 1:35)

Jesus had just spent time at Simon's home healing people, and many people had gathered there waiting for him to act. Where was he? Why was he not at the house, busy with the tasks at hand?

Jesus knew that time spent in prayer may look like doing nothing, but it is the most important thing we can do.

So take a deep breath and carve out some time to sit quietly in prayer. Spending time with God is never wasted time.

Wind

I woke up this morning to the sound of wind, a low humming that rose and fell in pitch and volume. I can't see the wind; the only evidence it exists is the tree's reaction to it—and that sound. Tornado and hurricane survivors speak of the sound of a freight train—powerful sounds, powerful forces, the wind.

From inside my home, I watch the barren tree limbs move as if by free will. They are dancing roundabout, back and forth, with no apparent purpose; and then they rest, as if tired from their exploits. The leaves on the magnolia tree shake and shiver. Then the sound picks up, and the dancing begins again.

Wind, breath, spirit. The Greeks and Romans envisioned wind as a god blowing air across the land. Simplistic to our twenty-first-century brains, and yet, isn't there something beyond our grasp in the wind? Isn't there something majestic and powerful and beyond our control?

> And suddenly from heaven came a sound like the rush
> of violent wind, and it filled the entire house where
> they were sitting. (Acts 2:2)

Wind can be a gentle breeze on a warm day, cooling and refreshing us. Wind can uproot trees and blow away buildings. The wind ushers in changes in weather and stills the sails in calm seas. Always changing, ever present, unpredictable, uncontrollable. Somewhat like God. We know it's there. We can feel it. We can hear it. We can see the results of its presence. But the wind does not operate at our beck and call, nor is it restricted by our expectations.

> The wind blows where it chooses, and you hear the
> sound of it, but you do not know where it comes from

> or where it goes. So it is with everyone who is born of the Spirit. (John 3:8)

We do know, two thousand years later, that wind is created when air particles move from high-pressure areas to low-pressure areas, and we know different air pressures result from variations in the way the sun heats the earth. Somehow this knowledge does not take the mystery and beauty and wonder out of the wind. Nor does this knowledge enable us to control the wind.

I believe in wind. I have felt it. I have heard it. I have seen the tree branches and leaves move, even if I can't see the actual wind. I know it can revive me on a hot day. I know it can harm me. A source of comfort, a source of change, a source of power.

I believe in God. I have felt His presence. I have heard Him whisper in my ear. I have seen obstacles and situations move and change, even if I can't see God. He revives me when I am burdened. He holds my fate in His hands. A source of comfort, a source of change, a source of power.

> In the beginning, when God created the heavens and the earth, the earth was a formless void and darkness covered the face of the deep, while a wind from God swept over the face of the waters. (Genesis 1:1–2)

I woke to the sound of wind this morning …

Why?

Years ago, I wanted a bigger house. Every time I prayed about it, I could hear the Spirit asking me, "Why?"

Like an insistent toddler, every answer I gave was followed by "Why?"

I wanted a bigger house because there wasn't enough room in this one. Why? We had so much stuff. Why? Because we needed all these things. Why? But everyone I know has a bigger house! Why does that matter?

Why? The question kept probing until I came to terms with some deeply held and formerly unchallenged attitudes. The question forced me to face some very uncomfortable truths about myself. Who was I trying to impress—God or my neighbors?

Before long, God seemed to pose this question before every endeavor I undertook. Why? I want to join this club. Why? I want to go to this party. Why? I want to volunteer here. Why? I want my kids to _____. Why?

> Beware of practicing your piety before others in order to be seen by them; for then you have no reward from your Father in heaven. So whenever you give alms, do not sound a trumpet before you, as the hypocrites do in the synagogues and in the streets, so that they may be praised by others. Truly I tell you, they have received their reward. (Matthew 6:1–2)

Does this mean I shouldn't have my name in the event program as a donor? Does this mean I shouldn't decide to donate more to be at the gold level? Why am I giving to this or that charity? Am I really committed to their work, or do I want to be a part of that crowd of people?

Why—it is the important question. Not why does God act the way He does, but why do I act the way I do? Self-examination is scary. It forces me to identify what and who I really value.

> Indeed, the word of God is living and active, sharper than any two-edged sword, piercing until it divides soul from spirit, joints from marrow; it is able to judge the thoughts and intentions of the heart. (Hebrews 4:12)

Years ago, I was in a Bible study on idols and false gods. We talked about what idols look like in today's world. I may not worship the statue of Athena, but I may worship knowledge. Many of us value what we have accomplished in this world, what we have made with our own hands. Have you seen Julie's new home? It is spectacular! And the new stadium for our football team? Wow! Very impressive.

> Their land is filled with silver and gold, and there is no end to their treasures; their land is filled with horses, and there is no end to their chariots. Their land is filled with idols; they bow down to the work of their own hands, to what their own fingers have made. (Isaiah 2:7–8)

There is nothing wrong with beautiful homes and state-of-the-art stadiums. There is nothing wrong, and many things that are right, with donating to worthy causes. There is nothing wrong, and many things that are right, about treasuring your family and friends.

The question becomes, do I value these things more than God? Am I honoring God with these things, or myself? The question becomes, why am I doing what I am doing? Why are you doing what you are doing?

That is something only you and God can determine. Only you can answer those whys for yourself, as only I can answer them for myself. God and His Spirit help me. He loves us so intensely. He desires our love in return.

> No one can serve two masters; for a slave will either hate the one and love the other, or be devoted to the one and despise the other. You cannot serve God and wealth. (Matthew 6:24)

Ask yourself, why?

Possibilities

I confess. I spent an hour the other day immersing myself in the new seed catalog. Oh, the possibilities! So many options! So many colors! So many different things that I could plant! They all look so beautiful, and I haven't even looked at the flowers yet!

> And Jesus said to them, "Take care! Be on your guard against all kinds of greed; for one's life does not consist in the abundance of possessions." (Luke 12:15)

Because let's be real here. I do not have the space, time, physical strength, or patience to grow all these plants. Some of them might not grow here even if I did have all those things. Professionals grew the fruit in these pictures, many different professionals from across the country. One hundred forty pages of fruits and vegetables and flowers, thousands of varieties. I will grow less than ten.

I am not a professional gardener; I am not even a very good gardener. To be good at something, truly good at it, takes time and effort and determination and commitment. I am not willing to give that to my garden.

Is this a lack of ambition on my part? A lack of seriousness? An aversion to hard work?

> A little sleep, a little slumber, a little folding of the hands to rest, and poverty will come upon you like a robber, and want, like an armed warrior. (Proverbs 6:10–11)

I like to think instead that I am dedicating my time, effort, and determination to other things, things I value more highly than giant bell peppers or cucumber varieties.

I like to think that I am not overcommitting myself to plants and a garden that will demand my time. I hope I am leaving ample space for God to lead me to new places, new activities, and other responsibilities.

As much as I love my garden, love being outside, love digging in the dirt, love harvesting fresh veggies, the garden is not my life, not my "small g" god. God is my God. If He were to call me away from the garden to other work, I hope I would go without a backward glance.

To keep myself open to the possibilities of what God may call me to do, I need to turn away from some of the possibilities presented to me by this catalog.

Overcommitment is something I have struggled with my entire life. I am not the only one. Keeping my hand down and my mouth shut often seems an impossible task. There is so much that needs doing, so much I could be doing. How do I balance doing too much with not doing enough?

It sounds simplistic, but first I must determine who I am letting judge what is too much and what is not enough. Am I comparing myself to a catalog of professional photos? Am I letting social media dictate how I should be spending my time? Am I trying to impress my friends?

> Am I now seeking human approval, or God's approval? Or am I trying to please people? If I were still pleasing people, I would not be a servant of Christ. (Galatians 1:10)

If I want to be a servant of Christ, and I do, then His approval is what I must seek. I need to focus on the activities He has given me to do. I need to sit at His feet and listen for what He wants me to do, then do it.

Just because the possibility exists for me to have a garden closer to the ones pictured in the catalog doesn't mean I should pursue it. Spending an hour looking at the pictures is like eye candy, garden porn, plant lust, I confess. I am grateful God calls me to turn my eyes away and return to Him.

> Set your minds on things that are above, not on things that are on earth. (Colossians 3:2)

Everything I Need

I have the space, the tiller, the fertilizer, and the fencing. I have the weed barrier, the seeds, and the plant food. I have the water source and the hose. I have cover to protect the young plants and support to help the growing ones. Now all I need is to actually start the garden.

While cleaning out the garage, I found bags of fertilizer and plant food. I had not realized that Nick had used either of these. It's no wonder the garden grew better under his care! Now I have some to add to my arsenal.

I have everything I need to grow a garden that will bear wonderful fruit. I just need to do it, because until I physically start a garden, all these tools aren't worth much. They are like a rubber band lying on the counter—unrealized potential.

> His divine power has given us everything needed for life and godliness. (2 Peter 1:3)

Everything I need for life and godliness.

God has given me this day, this time, His Spirit, His Word. God has given me an active church, Christian friends, Bible studies, and wise counselors. I trust the Holy Spirit to protect and support my growth.

I have been reading Robert J. Morgan's book on biblical meditation. He suggests many wonderful practices to deepen my relationship with God that I have never used. They seemed to have worked well for him. Now I can add them to my arsenal.

I have everything I need to grow in my relationship with God, Jesus, and the Holy Spirit. I just need to do it, because until I physically start praying, all these tools aren't worth much. They are like a rubber band lying on the counter—unrealized potential.

> But be doers of the word, and not merely hearers who deceive themselves. (James 1:22)

Those seeds need to be put in the ground; God's word needs to be written in my heart. Until that is done, I cannot expect to bear the fruit I so desperately want.

Do you want love? Joy? Peace? Patience? Would you like to respond to difficulties with kindness and gentleness? Would you like to be known for your generosity, faithfulness, and self-control? I would. I know I am not this way naturally. This is fruit that has to be grown.

> By contrast, the fruit of the Spirit is love, joy, peace, patience, kindness, generosity, faithfulness, gentleness, and self-control. (Galatians 5:22)

This is the fruit that God grows in my life through the Holy Spirit as I abide more and more with Jesus.

I want that fruit. I want a deeper relationship with God. I have everything I need.

To Grow or Not to Grow

"Are you going to grow tomatoes this year?" my friend asked.

A simple question, kindly asked by someone who knew that I have grown vegetables for the past thirty years. Well, my late husband and I grew them. My efforts and success since he passed away have been marginal.

Gardens are hard work. Not that I am opposed to hard work—it's just, well, hard. Gardens take manual labor and regular tending. You must set aside space in your yard and prepare the ground. You must commit to tending to the garden and providing what it needs to thrive.

Suddenly, the question was not about growing tomatoes, but about life and personal growth. Was I going to be open to growing something new in my life? Was I going to trust God?

Maybe not such a simple question after all.

> Whoever does not carry the cross and follow me cannot be my disciple. For which of you, intending to build a tower, does not first sit down and estimate the cost, to see whether he has enough to complete it? (Luke 14: 27–28)

I often battle inertia—the difficulty getting up off the couch and doing something. There are days I lose the battle. It's comfy on the couch.

I will battle inertia throughout the summer, along with predators who steal my seeds and fruit, weeds that stunt my plants' growth; and weather that can undo what progress I have made.

I battle these in my life as well. But God has granted me a vision of fresh vegetables where only barren ground now exists. And God has promised victory.

Are the results worth the battle? Delicious homegrown tomatoes, cucumbers, and sugar snaps—wow. A life full of family and friends—wow. Love, joy, peace, and patience—wow. A personal relationship with the Almighty—wow. Yep, they are worth getting off the couch.

> Again, the kingdom of heaven is like a merchant in search of fine pearls; on finding one pearl of great value, he went and sold all that he had and bought it. (Matthew 13:45–46)

Now to take that first step. If I want a garden, I must, at some point, actually go outside and plant something. If I want to continue in life, I must get off my comfy couch and do the tasks that need doing.

If I want a personal relationship with the Creator and master of the universe, I must at some point step outside my comfort zone and invite Him in. Such a relationship will not just happen, any more than fully ripe tomatoes will turn up without effort in my backyard.

And like a garden, like any relationship, it takes both of us. I need God to make the plant grow and bear fruit; He needs me to put the plant in the ground and water it.

> I am the vine, you are the branches. Those who abide in me and I in them bear much fruit, because apart from me you can do nothing. (John 15:5)

So yes, I *am* going to grow something this year, God willing. Are you?

Final Thoughts

What amazing gifts God has given me in the garden—fresh fruits and vegetables, insights into His nature, and lessons about life, all from getting my hands dirty.

I hope that you have been as blessed by reading these thoughts as I have been by writing them. God can grow beautiful things in our lives if we just give Him the time and space to do so.

I would like to encourage you to go outside today and look for God's presence.

He speaks to each of us in ways that words can never capture.

If you are looking for books that will help you deepen and strengthen your relationship with God, may I suggest *Reclaiming the Lost Art of Biblical Meditation* by Robert J. Morgan and *God Calling*, authors unknown, edited by A. J. Russell.

The best book for growing your relationship with God is the Bible. May I humbly suggest, however, that you come to the Bible with a heart and mind open to what the Spirit is teaching you. Without the Spirit's guidance, without the input of ministers and Bible scholars, the Bible can be confusing and contradictory. With the Spirit's guidance, the Bible is an amazing testimony to the power, grace, and love of God.

A special thank you to the readers and followers of my weekly blog, The Victory Garden. Thank you to my family and friends who have seen me through this process and encouraged me along the way. Thank you to First Presbyterian Church, Nashville, for nurturing my growth in Christ.

I would also like to thank WestBow Publishing for all their help in making this book a reality. Linda J. Beasley, my sister, created the illustrations in this book. I cannot thank her enough for the gifts of her time and talent.

There are not enough days to thank my God, who gave us His word and all growing things. I am eternally grateful for the gift of His son Jesus, who took on my sin so that I could be reconciled to Him, and for His Holy Spirit who guides my every step.

Thank you for reading these devotionals. If you would like more, please check out my weekly devotionals at www.thevictory.garden. I look forward to visiting with you in the garden!

Love in Christ,
Betsy S. Davies

About the Author

Betsy Davies lives beside a creek in Brentwood, Tennessee. She began writing a weekly devotional about her garden after her husband died. They had gardened together for thirty years; she is now learning to garden without him. Betsy's weekly devotionals combine her love of God with her love of gardening. You can find them at www.thevictory.garden.

Made in the USA
Monee, IL
25 June 2025